SIDE *by* SIDES

PRESTWICK HOUSE, INC.

MACBETH

WILLIAM SHAKESPEARE

Shakespeare's text

on the left;

modern rendering

on the right.

PRESTWICK
HOUSE
INCORPORATED

P.O. Box 246 • Cheswold, DE 19936
Tel: 1.800.932.4593
Web site: www.prestwickhouse.com

ISBN 1-58049-516-8

Table of Contents

CHARACTERS 5

ACT I
    SCENE 1 6
    SCENE 2 8
    SCENE 3 14
    SCENE 4 26
    SCENE 5 32
    SCENE 6 38
    SCENE 7 42

ACT II
    SCENE 1 48
    SCENE 2 54
    SCENE 3 62
    SCENE 4 76

ACT III
    SCENE 1 82
    SCENE 2 94
    SCENE 3 98
    SCENE 4 102
    SCENE 5 115
    SCENE 6 118

ACT IV
    SCENE 1 122
    SCENE 2 136
    SCENE 3 144

ACT V
    SCENE 1 164
    SCENE 2 170
    SCENE 3 174
    SCENE 4 180
    SCENE 5 182
    SCENE 6 188
    SCENE 7 190
    SCENE 8 194

STUDY GUIDE 202

4

DRAMATIS PERSONAE

DUNCAN, King of Scotland
MACBETH, Thane of Glamis and Cawdor, a general in the King's army
LADY MACBETH, his wife
MACDUFF, Thane of Fife, a nobleman of Scotland
LADY MACDUFF, his wife
MALCOLM, elder son of Duncan
DONALBAIN, younger son of Duncan
BANQUO, Thane of Lochaber, a general in the King's army
FLEANCE, his son
LENNOX, nobleman of Scotland
ROSS, nobleman of Scotland
MENTEITH, nobleman of Scotland
ANGUS, nobleman of Scotland
CAITHNESS, nobleman of Scotland
SIWARD, Earl of Northumberland, general of the English forces
YOUNG SIWARD, his son
SEYTON, attendant to Macbeth
HECATE, Queen of the Witches
The Three Witches
Boy, Son of Macduff
Gentlewoman attending on Lady Macbeth
An English Doctor
A Scottish Doctor
A Sergeant
A Porter
An Old Man
The Ghost of Banquo and other Apparitions
Lords, Gentlemen, Officers, Soldiers, Murderers, Attendants,
and Messengers

SCENE: Scotland and England

ACT I

SCENE 1
A desert place. Thunder and lightning.

[Enter three Witches.]

FIRST WITCH: When shall we three meet again?
  In thunder, lightning, or in rain?

SECOND WITCH: When the hurlyburly's done;
  When the battle's lost and won.

5 THIRD WITCH: That will be ere the set of sun.

FIRST WITCH: Where the place?

SECOND WITCH: Upon the heath.

THIRD WITCH: There to meet with Macbeth.

FIRST WITCH: I come, Graymalkin.

10 ALL: Paddock calls. Anon!
  Fair is foul, and foul is fair.
  Hover through the fog and filthy air.   *[Exeunt.]*

ACT I

SCENE 1
A deserted place. Thunder and lightning.

[Enter three Witches.]

FIRST WITCH: *Shall we three meet again when it is thundering, lightning, or raining?*

SECOND WITCH: *When the fighting's done; when the battle's lost and won.*

THIRD WITCH: *That will be before sunset.*

FIRST WITCH: *Where?*

SECOND WITCH: *Upon the heath.*

THIRD WITCH: *There we will meet with Macbeth.*

FIRST WITCH: *I come, my friend!*

ALL: *The toad calls. See you soon! Fair seems foul, and foul seems fair, through the fog and filthy air.*

[Exit.]

SCENE 2
A camp near Forres. Alarum within.

[Enter Duncan, Malcolm, Donalbain, Lennox, with Attendants, meeting a bleeding Sergeant.]

DUNCAN: What bloody man is that? He can report,
    As seemeth by his plight, of the revolt
    The newest state.

MALCOLM: This is the sergeant,
5   Who, like a good and hardy soldier fought
    'Gainst my captivity. Hail, brave friend!
    Say to the King the knowledge of the broil
    As thou didst leave it.

SERGEANT: Doubtful it stood,
10   As two spent swimmers that do cling together
    And choke their art. The merciless Macdonwald—
    Worthy to be a rebel, for to that
    The multiplying villainies of nature
    Do swarm upon him—from the western isles
15   Of kerns and gallowglasses is supplied;
    And fortune, on his damned quarrel smiling,
    Show'd like a rebel's whore, but all's too weak;
    For brave Macbeth—well he deserves that name—
    Disdaining fortune, with his brandish'd steel,
20   Which smoked with bloody execution,
    Like valor's minion carved out his passage
    Till he faced the slave,
    Which ne'er shook hands, nor bade farewell to him,
    Till he unseam'd him from the nave to the chaps,
25   And fix'd his head upon our battlements.

DUNCAN: O valiant cousin! Worthy gentleman!

SERGEANT: As whence the sun 'gins his reflection
    Shipwrecking storms and direful thunders break,

SCENE 2
A camp near Forres. Bell within.

[Enter Duncan, Malcolm, Donalbain, Lennox, with Attendants, meeting a bleeding sergeant.]

DUNCAN: *What bloody man is this? By his looks he can report the current news of the revolt.*

MALCOLM: *This is the sergeant who like a good and hardy soldier fought against my capture. Hail, brave friend! Tell the King your know-ledge of the fight as you left it.*

SERGEANT: *It was in a deadlock, like two tired swimmers that clutch each other, unable to swim together. The merciless Macdonwald—well-suited to be a rebel, in whom the multiplying evils of nature swarm, is supplied from Ireland with foot soldiers and heavy infantry. And Fortune seemed to smile on his rebel's cause. But to no avail; for brave Macbeth—well he deserves that name—disdaining Fortune, with his shining sword, which smoked with bloody execution, like Valor's favorite carved out his path until he faced Macdonwald. Without shaking hands or bidding him farewell, Macbeth cut him from the belly button to the chin and placed his severed head over our battlements.*

DUNCAN: *O, valiant cousin! Worthy gentleman!*

SERGEANT: *As from the east, where the sun rises but where shipwrecking storms and fearful thunders also begin, so also that*

30

So from that spring whence comfort seem'd to come
Discomfort swells. Mark, King of Scotland, mark:
No sooner justice had, with valor arm'd,
Compell'd these skipping kerns to trust their heels,
But the Norweyan lord, surveying vantage,
With furbish'd arms and new supplies of men,

35

Began a fresh assault.

DUNCAN: Dismay'd not this
Our captains, Macbeth and Banquo?

SERGEANT: Yes,
As sparrows eagles, or the hare the lion.

40

If I say sooth, I must report they were
As cannons overcharged with double cracks,
So they
Doubly redoubled strokes upon the foe.
Except they meant to bathe in reeking wounds,

45

Or memorize another Golgotha,
I cannot tell—
But I am faint; my gashes cry for help.

DUNCAN: So well thy words become thee as thy wounds;
They smack of honor both. Go get him surgeons.

[Exit Sergeant, attended.]

50

Who comes here?

[Enter Ross.]

MALCOLM: The worthy Thane of Ross.

LENNOX: What a haste looks through his eyes! So should he look
That seems to speak things strange.

ROSS: God save the King!

55

DUNCAN: Whence camest thou, worthy Thane?

spring which promised comfort swelled into our discomfort. Note, King of Scotland, note: no sooner had armed justice compelled these mercenaries to run from the battle, than the Norwegian lord, sensing an advantage, began a fresh assault with new supplies of men and stronger arms.

DUNCAN: *Did this dismay our generals, Macbeth and Banquo?*

SERGEANT: *Yes, as sparrows scare eagles, or the rabbit scares the lion. If I say honestly, I must report that they were like cannons overfilled with double charges. They doubled their strokes upon the enemy as if they meant to bathe in bloody wounds, or repeat another crucifixion, I cannot be sure which—but I am faint; my wounds cry for aid.*

DUNCAN: *Your words become you as do your wounds; they both smack of honor. Get him to the surgeons.*
                            [Exit Sergeant, attended.]
Who comes here?

[Enter Ross.]

MALCOLM: *The worthy lord of Ross.*

LENNOX: *What a hurried look in his eyes! So should one look who has to speak shocking things.*

ROSS: *God save the King!*

DUNCAN: *Where do you come from, worthy lord?*

Ross: From Fife, great King,
   Where the Norweyan banners flout the sky
   And fan our people cold.
   Norway himself, with terrible numbers,
60   Assisted by that most disloyal traitor
   The Thane of Cawdor, began a dismal conflict,
   Till that Bellona's bridegroom, lapp'd in proof,
   Confronted him with self-comparisons,
   Point against point rebellious, arm 'gainst arm,
65   Curbing his lavish spirit; and, to conclude,
   The victory fell on us.

Duncan: Great happiness!

Ross: That now
   Sweno, the Norways' king, craves composition;
70   Nor would we deign him burial of his men
   Till he disbursed, at Saint Colme's Inch,
   Ten thousand dollars to our general use.

Duncan: No more that Thane of Cawdor shall deceive
   Our bosom interest. Go pronounce his present death,
75   And with his former title greet Macbeth.

Ross: I'll see it done.

Duncan: What he hath lost, noble Macbeth hath won.

                                        [Exeunt.]

ROSS: *From Fife, great King, where the Norwegian banners scornfully fly and make our people fearful. The Norwegian king, with huge numbers and assisted by that most disloyal traitor, the lord of Cawdor, began a fierce conflict until Macbeth, dressed in armor, countered him blow for blow, sword against sword, and arm against arm, stopping his advance. And, to conclude, the victory is ours.*

DUNCAN: *Great happiness!*

ROSS: *Now Sweno, the Norwegian king, begs for a peace treaty; but we didn't allow him to bury his dead warriors until he paid, at Saint Colme's Island, ten thousand dollars for our general uses.*

DUNCAN: *No longer will the lord of Cawdor work against our intrest. Go announce his death immediately and give Macbeth his former title.*

ROSS: *I'll see that it is done.*

DUNCAN: *What he has lost, noble Macbeth has won.*

[Exit.]

SCENE 3
A heath.

[Thunder. Enter the three Witches.]

FIRST WITCH: Where hast thou been, sister?

SECOND WITCH: Killing swine.

THIRD WITCH: Sister, where thou?

FIRST WITCH: A sailor's wife had chestnuts in her lap,
5   And mounch'd, and mounch'd, and mounch'd.
"Give me," quoth I.
"Aroint thee, witch!" the rump-fed ronyon cries.
Her husband's to Aleppo gone, master o' the Tiger;
But in a sieve I'll thither sail,
10   And, like a rat without a tail,
I'll do, I'll do, and I'll do.

SECOND WITCH: I'll give thee a wind.

FIRST WITCH: Thou'rt kind.

THIRD WITCH: And I another.

15 FIRST WITCH: I myself have all the other,
And the very ports they blow,
All the quarters that they know
I' the shipman's card.
I will drain him dry as hay:
20   Sleep shall neither night nor day
Hang upon his penthouse lid;
He shall live a man forbid.
Weary se'n nights nine times nine
Shall he dwindle, peak, and pine;
25   Though his bark cannot be lost,
Yet it shall be tempest-tost.
Look what I have.

SCENE 3
A heath.

[Thunder. Enter the three Witches.]

FIRST WITCH: Where have you been, sister?

SECOND WITCH: I was killing pigs.

THIRD WITCH: Sister, where were you?

FIRST WITCH: A sailor's wife had chestnuts in her lap, and munched, and munched, and munched. "Give me some," said I. "Be gone, witch!" the garbage-fed pig cries. Her husband's gone to Aleppo, the master of the ship Tiger; but in a sieve I'll sail there, and, like a deformed rat, I'll do, I'll do, and I'll do.

SECOND WITCH: I'll give you a wind.

FIRST WITCH: You are kind.

THIRD WITCH: And I will give you another.

FIRST WITCH: I myself have all the rest, and I know the ports they visit, all the places that they know from the charts. I will drain him as dry as hay, and sleep will not visit his eyelids in daylight or night; he shall live a cursed man. For weeks on end he will be afflicted and hopeless; and though his boat cannot be lost, yet it shall be in terrible storms. Look what I have here.

SECOND WITCH: Show me, show me.

FIRST WITCH: Here I have a pilot's thumb,
30   Wreck'd as homeward he did come.

                                        [Drum within.]

THIRD WITCH: A drum, a drum!
      Macbeth doth come.

ALL: The weird sisters, hand in hand,
      Posters of the sea and land,
35   Thus do go about, about:
      Thrice to thine, and thrice to mine,
      And thrice again, to make up nine.
      Peace! The charm's wound up.

[Enter Macbeth and Banquo.]

MACBETH: So foul and fair a day I have not seen.

40   BANQUO: How far is't call'd to Forres? What are these
      So wither'd, and so wild in their attire,
      That look not like the inhabitants o' the earth,
      And yet are on't? Live you? or are you aught
      That man may question? You seem to understand me,
45   By each at once her choppy finger laying
      Upon her skinny lips. You should be women,
      And yet your beards forbid me to interpret
      That you are so.

MACBETH: Speak, if you can. What are you?

50   FIRST WITCH: All hail, Macbeth! hail to thee, Thane of Glamis!

SECOND WITCH: All hail, Macbeth! hail to thee, Thane of Cawdor!

THIRD WITCH: All hail, Macbeth, that shalt be King hereafter!

16

SECOND WITCH: *Show me, show me.*

FIRST WITCH: *Here I have a pilot's thumb, wrecked as he came homeward.*

[Drum within.]

THIRD WITCH: *A drum, a drum! Macbeth comes here.*

ALL: *The weird sisters, holding hands, travelers over the land and the sea, turn around and around; three times towards you and three times towards me, and three more until we make up nine. Peace! The spell is working.*

[Enter Macbeth and Banquo.]

MACBETH: *So foul and fair a day I have never seen.*

BANQUO: *How far is it to Forres?* [Referring to the witches.] *What are these so shriveled and so wildly dressed that they don't look like the inhabitants of the earth, and yet are on it? Are you alive? Can you understand my question? You seem to understand me, since each of you lays her scaly fingers upon her skinny lips. You should be women, and yet your whiskers stop me from concluding that you are.*

MACBETH: *Speak, if you can. What are you?*

FIRST WITCH: *All hail, Macbeth, hail to you, lord of Glamis!*

SECOND WITCH: *All hail, Macbeth, hail to you, lord of Cawdor!*

THIRD WITCH: *All hail, Macbeth, who shall be King in the future!*

BANQUO: Good sir, why do you start, and seem to fear
    Things that do sound so fair? I' the name of truth,
55   Are ye fantastical or that indeed
    Which outwardly ye show? My noble partner
    You greet with present grace and great prediction
    Of noble having and of royal hope,
    That he seems rapt withal. To me you speak not.
60   If you can look into the seeds of time,
    And say which grain will grow and which will not,
    Speak then to me, who neither beg nor fear
    Your favors nor your hate.

FIRST WITCH: Hail!

65 SECOND WITCH: Hail!

THIRD WITCH: Hail!

FIRST WITCH: Lesser than Macbeth, and greater.

SECOND WITCH: Not so happy, yet much happier.

THIRD WITCH: Thou shalt get kings, though thou be none.
70   So all hail, Macbeth and Banquo!

FIRST WITCH: Banquo and Macbeth, all hail!

MACBETH: Stay, you imperfect speakers, tell me more.
    By Sinel's death I know I am Thane of Glamis;
    But how of Cawdor? The Thane of Cawdor lives,
75   A prosperous gentleman; and to be King
    Stands not within the prospect of belief,
    No more than to be Cawdor. Say from whence
    You owe this strange intelligence, or why
    Upon this blasted heath you stop our way
80   With such prophetic greeting? Speak, I charge you.
                         [Witches vanish.]

BANQUO: *Good sir, why are you startled and why do you seem to fear these things that sound so wonderful?* [To witches.] *In the name of truth, are you spirits or women? You have greeted my noble partner with good news and great predictions of noble assets and of royal promise. He seems rapt with it all; to me you do not speak. If you can look into the seeds of time and predict which grain will grow and which will not, tell me my future, who neither begs nor fears either your favors or your hate.*

FIRST WITCH: *Hail!*

SECOND WITCH: *Hail!*

THIRD WITCH: *Hail!*

FIRST WITCH: *Lesser than Macbeth, but greater.*

SECOND WITCH: *Not as lucky, yet much luckier.*

THIRD WITCH: *Your children will be kings, but you will not be. Therefore, all hail Macbeth and Banquo!*

FIRST WITCH: *Banquo and Macbeth, all hail!*

MACBETH: *Stay, you imperfect speakers, tell me more. By the death of my father's kin I know that I am lord of Glamis; but how can I be of Cawdor? The lord of Cawdor lives and is a very prosperous gentleman. To be King is not a possibility, no more than to be lord of Cawdor is. Where did you get this strange information? Why upon this blasted place did you stop our passage with such prophetic greeting? Speak, I order you.*

[Witches vanish.]

BANQUO: The earth hath bubbles as the water has,
    And these are of them. Whither are they vanish'd?

MACBETH: Into the air, and what seem'd corporal melted
    As breath into the wind. Would they had stay'd!

85   BANQUO: Were such things here as we do speak about?
    Or have we eaten on the insane root
    That takes the reason prisoner?

MACBETH: Your children shall be kings.

BANQUO: You shall be King.

90   MACBETH: And Thane of Cawdor too. Went it not so?

BANQUO: To the selfsame tune and words. Who's here?

[Enter Ross and Angus.]

ROSS: The King hath happily received, Macbeth,
    The news of thy success; and when he reads
    Thy personal venture in the rebels' fight,
95   His wonders and his praises do contend
    Which should be thine or his. Silenced with that,
    In viewing o'er the rest o' the selfsame day,
    He finds thee in the stout Norweyan ranks,
    Nothing afeard of what thyself didst make,
100   Strange images of death. As thick as hail
    Came post with post, and every one did bear
    Thy praises in his kingdom's great defense,
    And pour'd them down before him.

ANGUS: We are sent
105   To give thee, from our royal master, thanks;
    Only to herald thee into his sight,
    Not pay thee.

20

BANQUO: *The earth has bubbles as the water does, and these creatures are of them. Where did they vanish to?*

MACBETH: *Into the air, and what seemed real vanished as breath does into the wind. I wish they would have stayed!*

BANQUO: *Were they really here, or have we eaten some hallucinogenic root that robs us of our reason?*

MACBETH: *Your children shall be kings.*

BANQUO: *You will be King.*

MACBETH: *And lord of Cawdor, too. Is that not how it went?*

BANQUO: *Precisely so. Who's here?*

[Enter Ross and Angus.]

ROSS: *The King has happily received, Macbeth, the news of your success; and when he calculated your personal part in this victory, he was hard pressed to separate his praise from what should be yours or his own. Speechless in viewing over the rest of the same day, he noted you striking the strong Norwegian ranks, not fearing what images of death you yourself caused. As thick as hail came messenger after messenger, and every one did speak your praises in our kingdom's great defense and poured them down before the King.*

ANGUS: *We are sent to give you thanks from our royal master. We are not here to reward you but only to usher you to him.*

ROSS: And for an earnest of a greater honor,
  He bade me, from him, call thee Thane of Cawdor.
110 In which addition, hail, most worthy Thane,
  For it is thine.

BANQUO: What, can the devil speak true?

MACBETH: The Thane of Cawdor lives. Why do you dress me
  In borrow'd robes?

115 ANGUS: Who was the Thane lives yet,
  But under heavy judgement bears that life
  Which he deserves to lose. Whether he was combined
  With those of Norway, or did line the rebel
  With hidden help and vantage, or that with both
120 He labor'd in his country's wreck, I know not;
  But treasons capital, confess'd and proved,
  Have overthrown him.

MACBETH: [Aside.] Glamis, and Thane of Cawdor!
  The greatest is behind. [To Ross and Angus.]
125 Thanks for your pains.   [Aside to Banquo.]
  Do you not hope your children shall be kings,
  When those that gave the Thane of Cawdor to me
  Promised no less to them?

BANQUO: [Aside to Macbeth.] That, trusted home,
130 Might yet enkindle you unto the crown,
  Besides the Thane of Cawdor. But 'tis strange;
  And oftentimes, to win us to our harm,
  The instruments of darkness tell us truths,
  Win us with honest trifles, to betray's
135 In deepest consequence—
  Cousins, a word, I pray you.

MACBETH: [Aside.] Two truths are told,
  As happy prologues to the swelling act
  Of the imperial theme!—I thank you, gentlemen.

Ross: *And, in promise of a greater honor, he asked me, from him, to call you lord of Cawdor. Hail, most worthy lord, for the title is yours!*

Banquo: *What, can the devil speak the truth?*

Macbeth: *The lord of Cawdor lives. Why do you clothe me in borrowed robes?*

Angus: *That man still lives, but he deserves to lose that life which he bears under deadly judgement. Whether he joined the Norwegians, supported the rebels with secret help, or both, I know not; but he did labor to destroy his country. He has been overthrown and his treasons confessed and proven.*

Macbeth: [Aside.] *Glamis, and lord of Cawdor! The greatest is to come.* [To Ross and Angus.] *Thanks for your pains.* [Aside to Banquo.] *Do you not hope your children will be kings when those that predicted I'd have the title of Cawdor promised no less to them?*

Banquo: [Aside to Macbeth.] *These certainties might light your ambition for the crown, besides the lord of Cawdor. But it is clear that often, to bring us to our destruction, the instruments of darkness tell us truths; they win us with honest trifles, in order to trick us into deepest consequences*—[To Angus and others.] *Cousins, a word, I ask you.*

Macbeth: [Aside.] *These two truths are told as happy prologues to the kingship. I thank you, gentlemen.* [Aside.] *This supernatural news cannot be bad or good. If it is bad, why would it have*

140   *[Aside.]* This supernatural soliciting
    Cannot be ill, cannot be good. If ill,
    Why hath it given me earnest of success,
    Commencing in a truth? I am Thane of Cawdor.
    If good, why do I yield to that suggestion
145   Whose horrid image doth unfix my hair
    And make my seated heart knock at my ribs,
    Against the use of nature? Present fears
    Are less than horrible imaginings:
    My thought, whose murder yet is but fantastical,
150   Shakes so my single state of man that function
    Is smother'd in surmise, and nothing is
    But what is not.

BANQUO: Look, how our partner's rapt.

MACBETH: *[Aside.]* If chance will have me king, why, chance may
                crown me,
155   Without my stir.

BANQUO: New honors come upon him,
    Like our strange garments, cleave not to their mould
    But with the aid of use.

MACBETH: *[Aside.]* Come what come may,
160   Time and the hour runs through the roughest day.

BANQUO: Worthy Macbeth, we stay upon your leisure.

MACBETH: Give me your favor; my dull brain was wrought
    With things forgotten. Kind gentlemen, your pains
    Are register'd where every day I turn
165   The leaf to read them. Let us toward the king.
    Think upon what hath chanced, and at more time,
    The interim having weigh'd it, let us speak
    Our free hearts each to other.

begun initially in a truth? I am lord of Cawdor. If good, why do I think about the horrid image which makes my hair stand on end and makes my heart knock at my ribcage unnaturally? My present fears are smaller than my horrible thoughts. Thoughts of possible murder shake my weakened state so that any action is smothered by thoughts of what's to come, and nothing is but what is not.

BANQUO: *Look, how our partner's deep in thought.*

MACBETH: [Aside.] *If luck will have me king, why, luck may crown me without my assistance.*

BANQUO: *New honors come upon him like new clothes, which only seem to fit after we get used to them.*

MACBETH: [Aside.] *No matter what happens, time moves through even the roughest day.*

BANQUO: *Worthy Macbeth, we wait for you.*

MACBETH: *I beg your pardon. My dull brain was filled with things I have forgotten. Kind gentlemen, your aid is recorded in my memory. Let us go toward the King.* [To Banquo.] *Think upon what has happened; and when we have more time, after weighing it all, let us speak freely to each other.*

BANQUO: Very gladly.

170 MACBETH: Till then, enough. Come, friends.

[Exeunt.]

SCENE 4
Forres. The palace.

[Flourish. Enter Duncan, Malcolm, Donalbain, Lennox, and Attendants.]

DUNCAN: Is execution done on Cawdor? Are not
    Those in commission yet return'd?

MALCOLM: My liege,
    They are not yet come back. But I have spoke
5   With one that saw him die, who did report
    That very frankly he confess'd his treasons,
    Implored your highness' pardon, and set forth
    A deep repentance. Nothing in his life
    Became him like the leaving it; he died
10   As one that had been studied in his death,
    To throw away the dearest thing he owed
    As 'twere a careless trifle.

DUNCAN: There's no art
    To find the mind's construction in the face:
15   He was a gentleman on whom I built
    An absolute trust.

BANQUO: *Very gladly.*

MACBETH: *Till then, enough. Come, friends.*

[Exit.]

SCENE 4
Forres. The palace.

[Flourish. Enter Duncan, Malcolm, Donalbain, Lennox, and Attendants.]

DUNCAN: *Has Cawdor been executed? Have those commissioned to do it returned?*

MALCOLM: *My King, they have not yet come back. But I have spoken to one who saw him die. He reported that the former lord confessed his treasons, asked your Highness' pardon, and expressed a deep repentance. Nothing in his life was done as honorably as his leaving it. He died calmly, as if he had rehearsed his death and it was unimportant.*

DUNCAN: *There's no way to judge a man's thoughts by his face. He was a gentleman I built an absolute trust upon.*

[Enter Macbeth, Banquo, Ross, and Angus.]

    O worthiest cousin!
    The sin of my ingratitude even now
    Was heavy on me. Thou art so far before,
20   That swiftest wing of recompense is slow
    To overtake thee. Would thou hadst less deserved,
    That the proportion both of thanks and payment
    Might have been mine! Only I have left to say,
    More is thy due than more than all can pay.

25 MACBETH: The service and the loyalty I owe,
    In doing it, pays itself. Your highness' part
    Is to receive our duties, and our duties
    Are to your throne and state, children and servants,
    Which do but what they should, by doing every thing
30   Safe toward your love and honor.

  DUNCAN: Welcome hither.
    I have begun to plant thee, and will labor
    To make thee full of growing. Noble Banquo,
    That hast no less deserved, nor must be known
35   No less to have done so; let me infold thee
    And hold thee to my heart.

  BANQUO: There if I grow,
    The harvest is your own.

  DUNCAN: My plenteous joys,
40   Wanton in fullness, seek to hide themselves
    In drops of sorrow. Sons, kinsmen, thanes,
    And you whose places are the nearest, know
    We will establish our estate upon
    Our eldest, Malcolm, whom we name hereafter
45   The Prince of Cumberland; which honor must
    Not unaccompanied invest him only,
    But signs of nobleness, like stars, shall shine
    On all deservers. From hence to Inverness,
    And bind us further to you.

[Enter Macbeth, Banquo, Ross, and Angus.]

O, worthiest cousin! I apologize for my ingratitude. You have deserved swifter payment than I have been able to give you. If you had deserved less, then all thanks and payment might have been mine! I can only say that more is your due than all of us can pay.

MACBETH: *The service and the loyalty I owe you in doing it pays for itself. Your Highness' job is to receive our duties, and our duties are to your throne and state, children and servants. We do only what we should—by doing everything well for your love and honor.*

DUNCAN: *Welcome here. I have begun to plant you and will - struggle to make you flourish. Noble Banquo, who deserves no less for all you have done; let me hug you and hold you to my heart.*

BANQUO: *If I grow there, the reward is yours.*

DUNCAN: *My great joys seek to hide themselves in tears.* [Wiping a tear from his eye.] *Sons, kinsmen, lords, and you who are nearest to me know that we will name our eldest son, Malcolm, the Prince of Cumberland; this honor must be accompanied by signs of nobleness, like stars which shine on all deserving. From here we shall travel to Inverness, and stay at Macbeth's castle; there we shall further strengthen our ties.*

50   MACBETH: The rest is labor, which is not used for you:
      I'll be myself the harbinger, and make joyful
      The hearing of my wife with your approach;
      So humbly take my leave.

  DUNCAN: My worthy Cawdor!

55   MACBETH: *[Aside.]* The Prince of Cumberland! That is a step
      On which I must fall down, or else o'erleap,
      For in my way it lies. Stars, hide your fires;
      Let not light see my black and deep desires:
      The eye wink at the hand; yet let that be
60   Which the eye fears, when it is done, to see.

                                        [Exit.]

  DUNCAN: True, worthy Banquo! He is full so valiant,
      And in his commendations I am fed;
      It is a banquet to me. Let's after him,
      Whose care is gone before to bid us welcome:
65   It is a peerless kinsman.

                              [Flourish. Exeunt.]

MACBETH: *My rest is labor which is not used for you. I'll be the messenger, and make my wife joyful at the news of your approach; so I humbly take my leave.*

DUNCAN: *My worthy lord of Cawdor!*

MACBETH: [Aside.] *This means that Malcom shall be the heir to the throne! That is an obstacle I must fall down upon or else leap over, for it lies in my way. Stars, hide your light; let not light see my wicked and deep desires. The eye winks at what the hand does, yet let that which the eye fears to see be done.*

[Exit.]

DUNCAN: *True, worthy Banquo! Macbeth is so full of bravery, that in his praises I am also fed; it is like a banquet to me. Let's go after him who has kindly gone before to bid us welcome. He is a peerless kinsman.*

[Flourish. Exit.]

SCENE 5
Inverness. Macbeth's castle.

[Enter Lady Macbeth, reading a letter.]

LADY MACBETH: "They met me in the day of success, and I have
learned by the perfectest report, they have more in them than mortal knowledge. When I burned in desire to question them further,
they made themselves air, into which they vanished. Whiles I stood
5   rapt in the wonder of it, came missives from the King, who all-
hailed me 'Thane of Cawdor'; by which title, before, these weird sisters saluted me, and referred me to the coming on of time with
'Hail, King that shalt be!' This have I thought good to deliver thee,
my dearest partner of greatness, that thou mightst not lose the dues
10 of rejoicing, by being ignorant of what greatness is promised thee.
Lay it to thy heart, and farewell."

Glamis thou art, and Cawdor, and shalt be
What thou art promised. Yet do I fear thy nature;
It is too full o' the milk of human kindness
15   To catch the nearest way. Thou wouldst be great;
Art not without ambition, but without
The illness should attend it. What thou wouldst highly,
That wouldst thou holily; wouldst not play false,
And yet wouldst wrongly win. Thou'ldst have, great Glamis,
20   That which cries, "Thus thou must do, if thou have it;
And that which rather thou dost fear to do
Than wishest should be undone." Hie thee hither,
That I may pour my spirits in thine ear,
And chastise with the valor of my tongue
25   All that impedes thee from the golden round,
Which fate and metaphysical aid doth seem
To have thee crown'd withal.

[Enter a Messenger.]

What is your tidings?

SCENE 5

Inverness. Macbeth's castle.

[Enter Lady Macbeth, reading a letter.]

LADY MACBETH: *"They met me on the day of victory, and I have learned by their perfect reports that they have more knowledge than mere mortals. When I burned in desire to question them still further, they made themselves like vapor and vanished. While I stood in wonder, messengers came from the King, who hailed me "Lord of Cawdor"; it was by this title the witches had saluted me and referred to future events with 'Hail, he who shall be king!' I thought it good to deliver this news, my dear partner of greatness, so that you might not lose your just rejoicing by being ignorant of what greatness also is promised you. Put it next to your heart and farewell."*

[Putting letter thoughtfully to her breast.]

You are lord of Glamis, and lord of Cawdor, and you shall be what you are promised. Yet I do fear your nature. It is too full of human compassion to hasten things the easiest way. You would be great and you are not without ambition, but you are without the ruthless nature you need. What you want most, you want to gain in a holy way; you would not do evil to win what you want. You would have the crown, husband, but you fear to do what needs doing. You are afraid of failure. Come here that I may pour my spirits into your ear, and remove by the power of my persuasion all that keeps you from the crown, which fate and supernatural aid seem to have alreadycrowned you.

[Enter a Messenger.]

What are your tidings?

MESSENGER: The King comes here tonight.

30 LADY MACBETH: Thou'rt mad to say it!
     Is not thy master with him? who, were't so,
     Would have inform'd for preparation.

   MESSENGER: So please you, it is true: our Thane is coming.
     One of my fellows had the speed of him,
35   Who, almost dead for breath, had scarcely more
     Than would make up his message.

   LADY MACBETH: Give him tending;
     He brings great news.   *[Exit Messenger.]*
     The raven himself is hoarse
40   That croaks the fatal entrance of Duncan
     Under my battlements. Come, you spirits
     That tend on mortal thoughts, unsex me here
     And fill me, from the crown to the toe, top-full
     Of direst cruelty! Make thick my blood,
45   Stop up the access and passage to remorse,
     That no compunctious visitings of nature
     Shake my fell purpose nor keep peace between
     The effect and it! Come to my woman's breasts,
     And take my milk for gall, you murdering ministers,
50   Wherever in your sightless substances
     You wait on nature's mischief! Come, thick night,
     And pall thee in the dunnest smoke of hell,
     That my keen knife see not the wound it makes,
     Nor heaven peep through the blanket of the dark
55   To cry, "Hold, hold!"

   [Enter Macbeth.]

     Great Glamis! Worthy Cawdor!
     Greater than both, by the all-hail hereafter!
     Thy letters have transported me beyond
     This ignorant present, and I feel now
60   The future in the instant.

MESSENGER: *The King comes here tonight.*

LADY MACBETH: *You are mad to say it! Is your master not with him? If it were the case, he would have told us to prepare.*

MESSENGER: *If it please you, it is true; our lord is coming. One of my men was quicker and almost out of breath. He scarcely had enough to give this message.*

LADY MACBETH: *Tend to him; he brings great news.*

[Exit Messenger.]

The raven himself croaks the fatal entrance of Duncan under my battlements. Come, spirits who tend on murderous thoughts, make me feel unsympathetic and fill me from head to toe with desperate cruelty! Make thick my blood; and stop up all access and passage to remorse so that no compassion will shake my savage purpose nor come between my intentions and their actions. Come to my woman's breasts and take my milk for vinegar, you murdering ministers, from wherever it is you wait on nature's mischief! Come, thick night, and wrap me in the murkiest smoke of hell so that my keen knife does not see the wound it makes, nor may heaven peep through the blanket of darkness to cry, "Stop, stop!"

[Enter Macbeth.]

Great Glamis! Worthy Cawdor! Made greater than both by the "all-hail" yet to come. Your letters have carried me beyond this ignorant present, and I feel now the entire future in this instant.

MACBETH: My dearest love,
   Duncan comes here tonight.

LADY MACBETH: And when goes hence?

MACBETH: Tomorrow, as he purposes.

65 LADY MACBETH: O, never
   Shall sun that morrow see!
   Your face, my Thane, is as a book where men
   May read strange matters. To beguile the time,
   Look like the time; bear welcome in your eye,
70   Your hand, your tongue; look like the innocent flower,
   But be the serpent under't. He that's coming
   Must be provided for; and you shall put
   This night's great business into my dispatch,
   Which shall to all our nights and days to come
75   Give solely sovereign sway and masterdom.

MACBETH: We will speak further.

LADY MACBETH: Only look up clear;
   To alter favor ever is to fear:
   Leave all the rest to me.

[Exeunt.]

MACBETH: My dearest love, Duncan comes here tonight.

LADY MACBETH: And when does he leave?

MACBETH: Tomorrow, as he proposes.

LADY MACBETH: O, never shall he see that morrow! Your face, my lord, is like a book where men may read strange matters. When they arrive, look as the occasion warrants; bear welcome in your eye, your hand, and your tongue. Look like an innocent flower but be the serpent under it. He that's coming must be taken care of; and you will put this night's great business into my hands, which shall have sole control over all our future nights and days.

MACBETH: We will speak further.

LADY MACBETH: Only look normally; show no fear in your expression; leave everything else to me.

[Exit.]

SCENE 6
Before Macbeth's castle. Hautboys and torches.

[Enter Duncan, Malcolm, Donalbain, Banquo, Lennox, Macduff, Ross, Angus, and Attendants.]

DUNCAN: This castle hath a pleasant seat; the air
    Nimbly and sweetly recommends itself
    Unto our gentle senses.

BANQUO: This guest of summer,
5   The temple-haunting martlet, does approve
    By his loved mansionry that the heaven's breath
    Smells wooingly here. No jutty, frieze,
    Buttress, nor coign of vantage, but this bird
    Hath made his pendant bed and procreant cradle;
10   Where they most breed and haunt, I have observed
    The air is delicate.

[Enter Lady Macbeth.]

DUNCAN: See, see, our honor'd hostess!
    The love that follows us sometime is our trouble,
    Which still we thank as love. Herein I teach you
15   How you shall bid God 'ild us for your pains,
    And thank us for your trouble.

LADY MACBETH: All our service
    In every point twice done, and then done double,
    Were poor and single business to contend
20   Against those honors deep and broad wherewith
    Your Majesty loads our house. For those of old,
    And the late dignities heap'd up to them,
    We rest your hermits.

SCENE 6

Before Macbeth's castle. Oboes and torches.

[Enter Duncan, Malcolm, Donalbain, Banquo, Lennox, Macduff, Ross, Angus, and Attendants.]

DUNCAN: *This castle has a pleasant disposition; the air here sweetly recommends itself to our calm senses.*

BANQUO: *This guest of summer, the church-loving martin, by his nesting proves that this castle has a pleasant scent. This bird has made his nests and cradles babies in every crack, crevice and structure. Where they breed and live, I have observed the air is most pleasant.*

[Enter Lady Macbeth.]

DUNCAN: *See, see, here's our honored hostess! The love you bear us and the love we bring causes you more work, which we still thank as love; and for the labor you bear in housing us we thank God for your pains and give thanks for your troubles.*

LADY MACBETH: *If all our service were done twice and then done doubly again, it would still be poor compared to those honors which your Majesty brings to our house; for those past ones and the new dignities heaped upon them, we are your humble servants.*

DUNCAN: Where's the Thane of Cawdor?
25   We coursed him at the heels and had a purpose
To be his purveyor; but he rides well,
And his great love, sharp as his spur, hath holp him
To his home before us. Fair and noble hostess,
We are your guest tonight.

30   LADY MACBETH: Your servants ever
Have theirs, themselves, and what is theirs, in compt,
To make their audit at your Highness' pleasure,
Still to return your own.

DUNCAN: Give me your hand;
35   Conduct me to mine host. We love him highly,
And shall continue our graces towards him.
By your leave, hostess.

[Exeunt.]

DUNCAN: *Where's the lord of Cawdor? We chased after him and had tried to arrive here first; but he rides well, and his great love, sharp as his spur, has helped him to his home before us. Fair and noble hostess, we are your guest tonight.*

LADY MACBETH: *As your servants, all we have in trust and account are your majesty's to audit and use as your own.*

DUNCAN: *Give me your hand; lead me to my host. We love him highly and shall continue our pledges towards him. With your permission, hostess.*

[Exit.]

SCENE 7
Macbeth's castle.

[Hautboys and torches. Enter a Sewer and divers Servants with dishes and service, who pass over the stage. Then enter Macbeth.]

MACBETH: If it were done when 'tis done, then 'twere well
It were done quickly. If the assassination
Could trammel up the consequence, and catch,
With his surcease, success; that but this blow
5   Might be the be-all and the end-all here,
But here, upon this bank and shoal of time,
We'd jump the life to come. But in these cases
We still have judgement here, that we but teach
Bloody instructions, which being taught return
10   To plague the inventor. This even-handed justice
Commends the ingredients of our poison'd chalice
To our own lips. He's here in double trust:
First, as I am his kinsman and his subject,
Strong both against the deed; then, as his host,
15   Who should against his murderer shut the door,
Not bear the knife myself. Besides, this Duncan
Hath borne his faculties so meek, hath been
So clear in his great office, that his virtues
Will plead like angels trumpet-tongued against
20   The deep damnation of his taking-off,
And pity, like a naked new-born babe,
Striding the blast, or heaven's cherubin horsed
Upon the sightless couriers of the air,
Shall blow the horrid deed in every eye,
25   That tears shall drown the wind. I have no spur
To prick the sides of my intent, but only
Vaulting ambition, which o'erleaps itself
And falls on the other.

[Enter Lady Macbeth.]

How now, what news?

SCENE 7
Macbeth's castle.

[Oboes and torches. Enter a Server and diverse Servants with dishes and service, who pass over the stage. Then enter Macbeth.]

MACBETH: *If it is to be done, it is better to do it quickly. If only the assassination and its consequences could end with Duncan's death; that only this blow might be the be-all and the end-all here. Then here, upon this bank and shoal of time, we would risk our future in heaven. But in such cases, we still may have to face judgment here; that we teach others how to kill, who having learned the lesson, return the instructions on our own bodies. He's here in double trust: first, as I am his relative and his subject, both are strong reasons not to do the deed. Also, as his host, I should stop any murderous plots, not bear the knife myself. Besides, this Duncan has carried his office so well, has been so wonderful in his great office, that his virtues will plead like trumpet-tongued angels against the deep damnation of his murder; and pity, like a new-born baby or heaven's angels, will force every eye to see the horrid deed so that their tears will drown the wind. I have no spur to goad my intentions, only vaulting ambition, which leaps over itself and lands on the other side.*

[Enter Lady Macbeth.]

Well! What news?

30   LADY MACBETH: He has almost supp'd. Why have you left the
        chamber?

MACBETH: Hath he ask'd for me?

LADY MACBETH: Know you not he has?

MACBETH: We will proceed no further in this business:
        He hath honor'd me of late, and I have bought
35   Golden opinions from all sorts of people,
        Which would be worn now in their newest gloss,
        Not cast aside so soon.

LADY MACBETH: Was the hope drunk
        Wherein you dress'd yourself? Hath it slept since?
40   And wakes it now, to look so green and pale
        At what it did so freely? From this time
        Such I account thy love. Art thou afeard
        To be the same in thine own act and valor
        As thou art in desire? Wouldst thou have that
45   Which thou esteem'st the ornament of life
        And live a coward in thine own esteem,
        Letting "I dare not" wait upon "I would"
        Like the poor cat i' the adage?

MACBETH: Prithee, peace!
50   I dare do all that may become a man;
        Who dares do more is none.

LADY MACBETH: What beast was't then
        That made you break this enterprise to me?
        When you durst do it, then you were a man;
55   And, to be more than what you were, you would
        Be so much more the man. Nor time nor place
        Did then adhere, and yet you would make both:
        They have made themselves, and that their fitness now
        Does unmake you. I have given suck, and know
60   How tender 'tis to love the babe that milks me:

LADY MACBETH: *He has almost finished eating. Why have you left the chamber?*

MACBETH: *Has he asked for me?*

LADY MACBETH: *Do you not know he has?*

MACBETH: *We will proceed no further in this business. He has honored me lately, and I have received golden opinions from all sorts of people; these should be displayed in their newest fashion, not cast aside so soon.*

LADY MACBETH: *What happened to the hope you had drunk in and wore? Has it slept since then? Does it wake now to look so sickly at what hope sought so freely? From this moment on, so I account your love. Are you afraid to be as valiant and courageous in action as you are in your desire? Would you wish to have the crown but live like a coward in your own life, letting "I dare not" smother "I wish," like the poor cat in the story who wanted to eat fish but was too afraid to wet its paws to get some?*

MACBETH: *Please, peace! I dare do all that may become a man; who dares to do more is no man.*

LADY MACBETH: *Then what was it that made you speak about this matter with me? When you dared to do it, then you were a man. And, to dare more than what you are, then you would be so much more. Neither time nor place were suitable, and yet you would make them so. They are suitable now, and their fitness now finds you unready. I have suckled babies and know how tender it is to love the babe that nurses—yet, I would, while it was smiling in my face, have plucked my nipple from its boneless gums and*

I would, while it was smiling in my face,
Have pluck'd my nipple from his boneless gums,
And dash'd the brains out, had I so sworn as you
Have done to this.

65   MACBETH: If we should fail?

LADY MACBETH: We fail!
But screw your courage to the sticking-place,
And we'll not fail. When Duncan is asleep—
Whereto the rather shall his day's hard journey
70   Soundly invite him—his two chamberlains
Will I with wine and wassail so convince,
That memory, the warder of the brain,
Shall be a fume and the receipt of reason
A limbec only. When in swinish sleep
75   Their drenched natures lie as in a death,
What cannot you and I perform upon
The unguarded Duncan? What not put upon
His spongy officers, who shall bear the guilt
Of our great quell?

80   MACBETH: Bring forth men-children only,
For thy undaunted mettle should compose
Nothing but males. Will it not be received,
When we have mark'd with blood those sleepy two
Of his own chamber, and used their very daggers,
85   That they have done't?

LADY MACBETH: Who dares receive it other,
As we shall make our griefs and clamor roar
Upon his death?

MACBETH: I am settled and bend up
90   Each corporal agent to this terrible feat.
Away, and mock the time with fairest show:
False face must hide what the false heart doth know.

[Exeunt.]

dashed its brains out if I had sworn to do this as you have sworn to me in this matter.

MACBETH: What if we should fail?

LADY MACBETH: We fail! But add your courage to commitment, and we'll not fail. When Duncan is asleep—which this day's hard journey soundly invites him to—I will give his two attendants so much wine that memory, the guardian of the brain, and reason shall be like a vapor and fade away. When in piggish sleep their drunken natures lie as if dead, what cannot you and I not perform upon the unguarded body of Duncan? What can we not pin on his drunken officers who will bear the guilt of our great murder?

MACBETH: Produce only male children, for your courageous nature should bear nothing else but males. Will it not be thought, once we have covered with blood those two sleepy guards, and used their very daggers, that they had committed the murder?

LADY MACBETH: Who would dare think otherwise, as we shall make our griefs and rages roar upon his death?

MACBETH: I am settled on the plan and commit to this terrible feat. Away, and mask the time with a show of sweetness. False faces will hide what our false hearts know.

[Exit.]

ACT II

SCENE 1
Inverness. Court of Macbeth's castle.

[Enter Banquo and Fleance, bearing a torch before him.]

BANQUO: How goes the night, boy?

FLEANCE: The moon is down; I have not heard the clock.

BANQUO: And she goes down at twelve.

FLEANCE: I take't 'tis later, sir.

5   BANQUO: Hold, take my sword. There's husbandry in heaven,
        Their candles are all out. Take thee that too.
        A heavy summons lies like lead upon me,
        And yet I would not sleep. Merciful powers,
        Restrain in me the cursed thoughts that nature
10   Gives way to in repose!

[Enter Macbeth and a Servant with a torch.]

        Give me my sword.
        Who's there?

MACBETH: A friend.

ACT II

SCENE 1
Inverness. Court of Macbeth's castle.

[Enter Banquo and his son Fleance, bearing a torch before him.]

BANQUO: *What's the time, boy?*

FLEANCE: *The moon is down; I have not yet heard the clock.*

BANQUO: *And the moon goes down at twelve.*

FLEANCE: *I believe it is later, sir.*

BANQUO: *Enough. Take my sword. There's economy in heaven, for the starry candles are all put out. Take that also. A heavy sleepiness lies like lead upon me, and yet I can not sleep. Merciful heavens, the cursed thoughts that nature puts in my head when I sleep!*

[Enter Macbeth and a Servant with a torch.]

Give me my sword. Who's there?

MACBETH: *A friend.*

BANQUO: What, sir, not yet at rest? The King's a-bed.
15   He hath been in unusual pleasure and
    Sent forth great largess to your offices:
    This diamond he greets your wife withal,
    By the name of most kind hostess, and shut up
    In measureless content.

20 MACBETH: Being unprepared,
    Our will became the servant to defect,
    Which else should free have wrought.

BANQUO: All's well.
    I dreamt last night of the three weird sisters:
25   To you they have show'd some truth.

MACBETH: I think not of them:
    Yet, when we can entreat an hour to serve,
    We would spend it in some words upon that business,
    If you would grant the time.

30 BANQUO: At your kind'st leisure.

MACBETH: If you shall cleave to my consent, when 'tis,
    It shall make honor for you.

BANQUO: So I lose none
    In seeking to augment it, but still keep
35   My bosom franchised and allegiance clear,
    I shall be counsell'd.

MACBETH: Good repose the while.

BANQUO: Thanks, sir, the like to you.

[Exeunt Banquo and Fleance.]

BANQUO: What, sir, are you not yet at rest? The King's in bed. He has been in an unusually good mood and sent forth great gifts to your people. This diamond he greets your wife with, calls her by the name of most kind hostess, and goes to bed in great contentment.

MACBETH: Being unprepared for him our abilities were not what we had hoped for. Otherwise I would feel content.

BANQUO: All's well. Last night I dreamed of the three weird sisters; to you they have showed some truth.

MACBETH: I don't think of them; yet, when we have an hour to spare, we could spend it in some words concerning that business if you would grant me the time.

BANQUO: At your kindest leisure.

MACBETH: If you shall join with me at that time, it shall make honor for you.

BANQUO: If I don't lose any honor in seeking to implement it, and I still keep my allegiance clear, and heart guiltless, I shall be advised.

MACBETH: Have a good evening!

BANQUO: Thanks, sir, the same to you.

[Exit Banquo. and Fleance.]

MACBETH: Go bid thy mistress, when my drink is ready,
She strike upon the bell. Get thee to bed.

[Exit Servant.]

40   Is this a dagger which I see before me,
The handle toward my hand? Come, let me clutch thee.
I have thee not, and yet I see thee still.
Art thou not, fatal vision, sensible
To feeling as to sight? Or art thou but
45   A dagger of the mind, a false creation,
Proceeding from the heat-oppressed brain?
I see thee yet, in form as palpable
As this which now I draw.
Thou marshall'st me the way that I was going,
50   And such an instrument I was to use.
Mine eyes are made the fools o' the other senses,
Or else worth all the rest. I see thee still,
And on thy blade and dudgeon gouts of blood,
Which was not so before. There's no such thing:
55   It is the bloody business which informs
Thus to mine eyes. Now o'er the one half-world
Nature seems dead, and wicked dreams abuse
The curtain'd sleep; witchcraft celebrates
Pale Hecate's offerings; and wither'd Murder,
60   Alarum'd by his sentinel, the wolf,
Whose howl's his watch, thus with his stealthy pace,
With Tarquin's ravishing strides, towards his design
Moves like a ghost. Thou sure and firm-set earth,
Hear not my steps, which way they walk, for fear
65   Thy very stones prate of my whereabout,
And take the present horror from the time,
Which now suits with it. Whiles I threat, he lives;
Words to the heat of deeds too cold breath gives.

[A bell rings.]

I go, and it is done: the bell invites me.
70   Hear it not, Duncan, for it is a knell
That summons thee to heaven, or to hell.

[Exit.]

MACBETH: *Go bid your mistress to strike upon the bell when my drink is ready. Then get to bed.*

[Exit Servant.]

[His gaze suddenly arrested by a sight across the room.]

Is this a dagger that I see in front of me with the handle toward my hand? Come, let me clutch you. [Reaches for the dagger he imagines.] *I don't have you, and yet I still see you. Fatal vision, are you not as real to feeling as to sight? Or are you only an imaginary dagger, a false illusion coming from the heat-oppressed brain? I see you yet, in form as real as this one which I now draw. You lead me in the direction that I was going, and such an instrument as this was I to use. My eyes are made the fool by the other senses. I see you still, and on my blade and hand are drops of blood which were not there before. This is not real. It is the murderous business which tricks my eyes. Now in one half the world nature seems dead, and while wicked dreams abuse sleep, witchcraft celebrates its queen's offerings; and withered Murder, alarmed by his sentinel, the wolf (whose howls mark his watch) moves with his silent pace, like a ghost, toward his purpose. You, firm earth, do not hear my steps nor the stealthy way in which I move, for fear the very stones will tell of my whereabouts and take the horror from this time, which now suits it perfectly. But while I threaten, Duncan lives; these too cold words delay me from my hot deeds.*

[A bell rings.]

I go, and it is done; the bell invites me to the crime. Do not hear it, Duncan, for it is a sound that summons you to heaven, or to hell.

[Exit.]

53

SCENE 2
The same.

[Enter Lady Macbeth.]

LADY MACBETH: That which hath made them drunk hath made me
    bold;
  What hath quench'd them hath given me fire. Hark! Peace!
  It was the owl that shriek'd, the fatal bellman,
  Which gives the stern'st good-night. He is about it:
5   The doors are open, and the surfeited grooms
  Do mock their charge with snores: I have drugg'd their possets,
  That death and nature do contend about them,
  Whether they live or die.

MACBETH: *[Within.]* Who's there? what, ho!

10 LADY MACBETH: Alack, I am afraid they have awaked
  And 'tis not done. The attempt and not the deed
  Confounds us. Hark! I laid their daggers ready;
  He could not miss 'em. Had he not resembled
  My father as he slept, I had done't.

[Enter Macbeth.]
15   My husband!

MACBETH: I have done the deed. Didst thou not hear a noise?

LADY MACBETH: I heard the owl scream and the crickets cry.
  Did not you speak?

MACBETH: When?

20 LADY MACBETH: Now.

MACBETH: As I descended?

SCENE 2
The same.

[Enter Lady Macbeth.]

LADY MACBETH: *The wine that has made them drunk has made me bold; what has silenced them has filled me with fire. What! Peace! That was the owl, the bellringer whose shriek marks the night. Macbeth is doing it. The doors are open, and the stuffed grooms tend to their job with only snores. I have drugged their drinks so that death and nature swirl around them, deciding if they live or die.*

MACBETH: [Within.] *Who's there? What, hello!*

LADY MACBETH: *Alas, I am afraid that the grooms have awakened and the deed is not yet done. The unsuccessful attempt and not the deed itself ruins us. What! I laid their daggers ready. Macbeth could not have missed them. If, as he slept, Duncan had not resembled my father I would have done it.*

[Enter Macbeth.]
  My husband!

MACBETH: *I have completed the deed. Did you not hear a noise?*

LADY MACBETH: *I heard only the owl scream and the crickets cry. Did you not speak?*

MACBETH: *When?*

LADY MACBETH: *Now.*

MACBETH: *As I descended?*

LADY MACBETH: Ay.

MACBETH: Hark!
    Who lies i' the second chamber?

25   LADY MACBETH: Donalbain.

MACBETH: This is a sorry sight.   *[Looks on his hands.]*

LADY MACBETH: A foolish thought, to say a sorry sight.

MACBETH: There's one did laugh in's sleep, and one cried, "Murder!"
    That they did wake each other: I stood and heard them:
30   But they did say their prayers and address'd them
    Again to sleep.

LADY MACBETH: There are two lodged together.

MACBETH: One cried, "God bless us!" and "Amen" the other,
    As they had seen me with these hangman's hands.
35   Listening their fear, I could not say "Amen,"
    When they did say "God bless us!"

LADY MACBETH: Consider it not so deeply.

MACBETH: But wherefore could not I pronounce "Amen"?
    I had most need of blessing, and "Amen"
40   Stuck in my throat.

LADY MACBETH: These deeds must not be thought
    After these ways; so, it will make us mad.

MACBETH: Me thought I heard a voice cry "Sleep no more!
    Macbeth doth Murder sleep" —the innocent sleep,
45   Sleep that knits up the ravell'd sleave of care,
    The death of each day's life, sore labor's bath,
    Balm of hurt minds, great nature's second course,
    Chief nourisher in life's feast—

LADY MACBETH: *Yes.*

MACBETH: *Listen! Who lies in the second room?*

LADY MACBETH: *Donalbain.*

MACBETH: *This is an awful sight.*
                    [Looks on his hands.]

LADY MACBETH: *It is a foolish thought, to say an awful sight.*

MACBETH: *One of the grooms laughed in his sleep, and the other one cried "Murder!" They woke each other; I stood and heard them. But they said their prayers again and settled into sleep once more.*

LADY MACBETH: *There are two roomed together.*

MACBETH: *One cried, "God bless us!" and the other said "Amen," as if they had seen me with these bloody hands. Listening to their fears, I could not say "Amen," when they said, "God bless us!"*

LADY MACBETH: *Do not think about it so deeply.*

MACBETH: *Why could I not pronounce "Amen"? I had a great need for blessing, and "Amen" stuck in my throat.*

LADY MACBETH: *You must not think about these deeds like this, or else we shall go mad.*

MACBETH: *I thought I heard a voice cry "Sleep no more! Macbeth does murder sleep," —innocent sleep, sleep that ties up all our cares, sleep, which is death to each day's life, sleep, a soothing bath for the day's strenuous labor and a balm for hurt minds; sleep, a great second course of nourishment for life's feast—*

57

LADY MACBETH: What do you mean?

50   MACBETH: Still it cried, "Sleep no more!" to all the house;
        "Glamis hath murdered sleep, and therefore Cawdor
        Shall sleep no more. Macbeth shall sleep no more."

LADY MACBETH: Who was it that thus cried? Why, worthy Thane,
        You do unbend your noble strength, to think
55   So brainsickly of things. Go, get some water
        And wash this filthy witness from your hand.
        Why did you bring these daggers from the place?
        They must lie there. Go carry them, and smear
        The sleepy grooms with blood.

60   MACBETH: I'll go no more:
        I am afraid to think what I have done;
        Look on't again I dare not.

LADY MACBETH: Infirm of purpose!
        Give me the daggers. The sleeping and the dead
65   Are but as pictures; 'tis the eye of childhood
        That fears a painted devil. If he do bleed,
        I'll gild the faces of the grooms withal,
        For it must seem their guilt.

[Exit. Knocking within.]

MACBETH: Whence is that knocking?
70   How is't with me, when every noise appals me?
        What hands are here? Ha, they pluck out mine eyes!
        Will all great Neptune's ocean wash this blood
        Clean from my hand? No, this my hand will rather
        The multitudinous seas incarnadine,
75   Making the green one red.

[Re-enter Lady Macbeth.]

LADY MACBETH: *What do you mean?*

MACBETH: *Still it cried, "Sleep no more!" to all the house; "The lord of Glamis has murdered sleep, and therefore, the lord of Cawdor shall sleep no more. Macbeth shall sleep no more."*

LADY MACBETH: *Who was it who thus cried? Worthy lord, you dissolve your noble strength by thinking of such sickly things. Go get some water and wash this bloody evidence from your hands. Why did you bring those daggers from the room? They must lie there. Go return them, and smear the sleepy grooms with the blood.*

MACBETH: *I'll go no more. I am afraid to think about what I have done; I dare not look on it again.*

LADY MACBETH: *Yur will is weak! Give me the daggers. The sleeping and the dead are only like pictures. It is childishness to fear a painted devil. If Duncan bleeds, I'll cover the faces of the grooms with it; for it must seem their guilt.*

[Exit. Knocking within.]

MACBETH: *Where is that knocking coming from? How is it with me that every single noise appalls me? What are these hands here? Ah! They destroy my eyes. Can all of the great oceans waters cleanse this blood from my hands? No, my hand will instead redden the vast seas, making the green sea one of red.*

[Re-enter Lady Macbeth.]

LADY MACBETH: My hands are of your color, but I shame
  To wear a heart so white. *[Knocking within.]*
  I hear a knocking
  At the south entry. Retire we to our chamber.
80 A little water clears us of this deed:
  How easy is it then! Your constancy
  Hath left you unattended. *[Knocking within.]*
  Hark! more knocking:
  Get on your nightgown, lest occasion call us
85 And show us to be watchers. Be not lost
  So poorly in your thoughts.

MACBETH: To know my deed, 'twere best not know myself.
                    [Knocking within.]
  Wake Duncan with thy knocking! I would thou couldst!

                              [Exeunt.]

LADY MACBETH: *My hands are of your color, but I am ashamed to wear a heart so white.* [Knocking within.] *I hear a knocking at the south gate; we need to go to our room. A little water clears us of this deed. How easy it is! Your composure has left you.* [Knocking within.] *Listen! More knocking. Get on your night-clothes so that if we are called we will not appear to have been awake. Do not be lost in your own thoughts.*

MACBETH: *Knowing my deed, I would rather not know myself.*
[Knocking within.]
Wake Duncan with your knocking! I wish you could!

[Exit.]

SCENE 3
The same.

[Enter a Porter. Knocking within.]

PORTER: Here's a knocking indeed! If a man were porter of hell-gate, he should have old turning the key.
[Knocking within.]
Knock, knock, knock! Who's there, i' the name of Belzebub? Here's a farmer that hanged himself on th' expectation of plenty. Come in
5   time! Have napkins enow about you; here you'll sweat for't. *[Knocking within.]* Knock, knock! Who's there, in th' other devil's name? Faith, here's an equivocator that could swear in both the scales against either scale, who committed treason enough for God's sake, yet could not equivocate to heaven. O, come in, equivocator.
10   *[Knocking within.]* Knock, knock, knock! Who's there? Faith, here's an English tailor come hither, for stealing out of a French hose. Come in, tailor; here you may roast your goose. *[Knocking within.]* Knock, knock! Never at quiet! What are you? But this place is too cold for hell. I'll devil-porter it no further. I had thought to have let
15   in some of all professions, that go the primrose way to the everlasting bonfire. *[Knocking within.]* Anon, anon! I pray you, remember the porter.   *[Opens the gate.]*

[Enter Macduff and Lennox.]

MACDUFF: Was it so late, friend, ere you went to bed,
    That you do lie so late?

20 PORTER: Faith, sir, we were carousing till the second cock: and drink, sir, is a great provoker of three things.

MACDUFF: What three things does drink especially provoke?

PORTER: Marry, sir, nose-painting, sleep, and urine. Lechery, sir, it provokes and unprovokes: it provokes the desire, but it takes away the

62

SCENE 3
The same.

[Enter a Porter aroused by the knocking. As he walks toward the gate he can be heard to mutter.]

PORTER: *There's a knocking indeed! If a man were gatekeeper of hell, he should have plenty of work.* [Knocking within.] *Knock, knock, knock! Who's there, in the name of the devil? Here's a farmer who hanged himself by trying to get rich quickly. Come in, have plenty of towels with you; here you'll sweat for it.* [Knocking within.] *Knock, knock! Who's there, in the other devil's name? Indeed, here's a priest who could swear on both sides of an issue against either side; he committed treason for God's sake, yet he could not talk his way into heaven. O, come in, big talker.* [Knocking within.] *Knock, knock, knock! Who's there? Well, here's an English tailor who comes here for stealing cloth. Come in tailor; here you will roast your goose.* [Knocking within.] *Knock, knock; this place is never quiet! What are you? But this place is too cold for hell. I'll no longer devil-porter it. I had thought I would let in some from all professions that travel the path of pleasure and end up in hell.* [Knocking within.] *Wait, wait! I pray you, remember the gatekeeper.* [Opens the gate.]

[Enter Macduff and Lennox.]

MACDUFF: *Did you stay up so long, friend, that you are still asleep so late this morning?*

PORTER: *Faith, sir, we were partying until three; and drink, sir, is a great stimulator of three things.*

MACDUFF: *What three things does drink especially provoke?*

PORTER: *Well, sir, red noses, sleep, and urination. Sexual thoughts, sir, it provokes and unprovokes. It stimulates the desire, but it*

25 performance. Therefore much drink may be said to be an equivocator with lechery: it makes him, and it mars him; it sets him on and it takes him off; it persuades him and disheartens him; makes him stand to and not stand to; in conclusion, equivocates him in a sleep, and giving him the lie, leaves him.

30 MACDUFF: I believe drink gave thee the lie last night.

PORTER: That it did, sir, i' the very throat on me: but I requited him for his lie, and, I think, being too strong for him, though he took up my legs sometime, yet I made a shift to cast him.

MACDUFF: Is thy master stirring?

[Enter Macbeth.]
35 Our knocking has awaked him; here he comes.

LENNOX: Good morrow, noble sir.

MACBETH: Good morrow, both.

MACDUFF: Is the King stirring, worthy Thane?

MACBETH: Not yet.

40 MACDUFF: He did command me to call timely on him;
I have almost slipp'd the hour.

MACBETH: I'll bring you to him.

MACDUFF: I know this is a joyful trouble to you;
But yet 'tis one.

45 MACBETH: The labor we delight in physics pain.
This is the door.

takes away the performance. Therefore, much drink may be said to be unfair to lust. It makes him desirous but makes him inefficient; it leads him on and it makes him weak; it persuades him and disheartens him; it makes him stand tall and not stand at all. In conclusion, drink tricks him into sleeping and leaves him with only dreams.

MACDUFF: I believe drink got the better of you last night.

PORTER: That it did, sir, in my very throat. But I paid him back for his lie; and, I think, I was too strong for him. He almost bested me, but I was finally able to throw him up.

MACDUFF: Is your master stirring?

[Enter Macbeth.]
   Our knocking woke him; here he comes.

LENNOX: Good morning, noble sir.

MACBETH: Good morning to you both.

MACDUFF: Is the King up yet, worthy lord?

MACBETH: Not yet.

MACDUFF: He commanded me to call on him early, and I am running late.

MACBETH: I'll bring you to him.

MACDUFF: I know this may be a joyful trouble to you, but it is still a trouble.

MACBETH: The labor we delight in cures such pain. This is the door.

MACDUFF: I'll make so bold to call,
For 'tis my limited service.

[Exit.]

LENNOX: Goes the King hence today?

50 MACBETH: He does: he did appoint so.

LENNOX: The night has been unruly. Where we lay,
Our chimneys were blown down, and, as they say,
Lamentings heard i' the air, strange screams of death,
And prophesying with accents terrible
55 Of dire combustion and confused events
New hatch'd to the woeful time. The obscure bird
Clamor'd the livelong night. Some say the earth
Was feverous and did shake.

MACBETH: 'Twas a rough night.

60 LENNOX: My young remembrance cannot parallel
A fellow to it.

[Re-enter Macduff.]

MACDUFF: O horror, horror, horror! Tongue nor heart
Cannot conceive nor name thee.

MACBETH: ⎫
65 LENNOX: ⎭ What's the matter?

MACDUFF: Confusion now hath made his masterpiece.
Most sacrilegious Murder hath broke ope
The Lord's anointed temple and stole thence
The life o' the building.

70 MACBETH: What is't you say? the life?

66

MACDUFF: *I'll be so bold as to call, for it is my small duty.*

[Exit.]

LENNOX: *Does the King leave today?*

MACBETH: *He does; he did arrange for it.*

LENNOX: *The night has been very rough. Near our camp chimneys were blown down; and, as some say, strange screams of death filled the air prophesying confused events and terrible acts newly hatched in this woeful time. The owl screeched the livelong night. Some say the earth was feverish and did shake.*

MACBETH: *It was a rough night.*

LENNOX: *In my few years of life, I cannot remember as rough a one.*

[Re-enter an Macduff.]

MACDUFF: *O horror, horror, horror! Neither tongue nor heart can name this horror!*

MACBETH:
LENNOX: } *What's the matter?*

MACDUFF: *Confusion has now made his masterpiece! The most sacrilegious murder has broken open our Lord's holy temple and stolen his life.*

MACBETH: *What is it you say? The life?*

67

LENNOX: Mean you his Majesty?

MACDUFF: Approach the chamber, and destroy your sight
　　With a new Gorgon. Do not bid me speak;
　　See, and then speak yourselves.

　　　　　　　　　　　　[Exeunt Macbeth and Lennox.]

75　　Awake, awake!
　　Ring the alarum bell. Murder and treason!
　　Banquo and Donalbain! Malcolm, awake!
　　Shake off this downy sleep, death's counterfeit,
　　And look on death itself! Up, up, and see
80　　The great doom's image! Malcolm! Banquo!
　　As from your graves rise up, and walk like sprites,
　　To countenance this horror! Ring the bell.

　　　　　　　　　　　　　　　　[Bell rings.]

[Enter Lady Macbeth.]

LADY MACBETH: What's the business,
　　That such a hideous trumpet calls to parley
85　　The sleepers of the house? Speak, speak!

MACDUFF: O gentle lady,
　　'Tis not for you to hear what I can speak:
　　The repetition in a woman's ear
　　Would murder as it fell.

[Enter Banquo.]

90　　O Banquo, Banquo!
　　Our royal master's murdered.

LADY MACBETH: Woe, alas!
　　What, in our house?

BANQUO: Too cruel any where.
95　　Dear Duff, I prithee, contradict thyself,
　　And say it is not so.

68

LENNOX: *Do you mean his Majesty?*

MACDUFF: *Approach the chamber and destroy your eyes with a sight as terrible as the sight of. Do not ask me to speak further. See it, and then speak yourselves.*

[Exit Macbeth and Lennox.]

Awake, awake! Ring the alarm bell. Murder and treason! Banquo and Donalbain! Malcolm, awake! Shake off death's counterfeit, sleep, and look upon death itself! Up, up, and see the image of Doomsday! Malcolm! Banquo! Rise up from your graves to witness this horror! Ring the bell.

[Bell rings.]

[Enter Lady Macbeth.]

LADY MACBETH: *What's this business that such a hideous trumpet calls everyone to wake up? Speak, speak!*

MACDUFF: *O, gentle lady, what I have to speak is too harsh for you to hear. Spoken in a woman's ear, it would murder the woman who heard it.*

[Enter Banquo.]

O, Banquo, Banquo! Our royal master's murdered.

LADY MACBETH: *Woe, alas! What in our house?*

BANQUO: *It would be too cruel anywhere. Macduff, I ask you to correct yourself and say it is not so.*

[Re-enter Macbeth and Lennox, with Ross.]

MACBETH: Had I but died an hour before this chance,
    I had lived a blessed time; for from this instant
    There's nothing serious in mortality:
100   All is but toys; renown and grace is dead;
    The wine of life is drawn, and the mere lees
    Is left this vault to brag of.

[Enter Malcolm and Donalbain.]

DONALBAIN: What is amiss?

MACBETH: You are, and do not know't:
105   The spring, the head, the fountain of your blood
    Is stopp'd; the very source of it is stopp'd.

MACDUFF: Your royal father's murdered.

MALCOLM: O, by whom?

LENNOX: Those of his chamber, as it seem'd, had done't:
110   Their hands and faces were all badged with blood;
    So were their daggers, which unwiped we found
    Upon their pillows:
    They stared, and were distracted; no man's life
    Was to be trusted with them.

115 MACBETH: O, yet I do repent me of my fury,
    That I did kill them.

MACDUFF: Wherefore did you so?

MACBETH: Who can be wise, amazed, temperate and furious,
    Loyal and neutral, in a moment? No man:
120   The expedition of my violent love
    Outrun the pauser reason. Here lay Duncan,
    His silver skin laced with his golden blood,
    And his gash'd stabs look'd like a breach in nature

[Re-enter Macbeth and Lennox, with Ross.]

MACBETH: *If I died only an hour ago, I would have lived a blessed life; but from this moment there's nothing serious in mortality: everything is trivial; fame and grace are dead; the wine of life is drained, and all that is left is the residue.*

[Enter Malcolm and Donalbain.]

DONALBAIN: *What is wrong?*

MACBETH: *You are, and do not know it. The spring, the head, the fountain of your blood is stopped; the very source of it is has been stopped.*

MACDUFF: *Your royal father is murdered.*

MALCOLM: *Oh, by whom?*

LENNOX: *It seems that his attendants have done it. Their hands and faces were all marked with blood as were their daggers, which we found all bloody on their pillows. They stared and looked insane; no man's life was to be trusted with them.*

MACBETH: *O, yet I do repent of my fury that made me kill them.*

MACDUFF: *Why did you do that?*

MACBETH: *Who can be wise, amazed, controlled and furious, loyal and neutral, all in an instant? No one can. The speed of my violent love for Duncan outran reason. Here lay Duncan, his silvery skin laced with his golden blood; and his gashed stabs looked like a breach in nature, allowing for the entrance of ruin. And there were the murderers, covered in the colors of their trade,*

For ruin's wasteful entrance: there, the murderers,
125 Steep'd in the colors of their trade, their daggers
Unmannerly breech'd with gore. Who could refrain,
That had a heart to love, and in that heart
Courage to make's love known?

LADY MACBETH: Help me hence, ho!

130 MACDUFF: Look to the lady.

MALCOLM: [Aside to Donalbain.] Why do we hold our   tongues,
That most may claim this argument for ours?

DONALBAIN: [Aside to Malcolm.] What should be spoken here, where
our fate,
Hid in an auger-hole, may rush and seize us?
135 Let's away;
Our tears are not yet brew'd.

MALCOLM: [Aside to Donalbain.] Nor our strong sorrow
Upon the foot of motion.

BANQUO: Look to the lady:
[Lady Macbeth is carried out.]
140 And when we have our naked frailties hid,
That suffer in exposure, let us meet
And question this most bloody piece of work
To know it further. Fears and scruples shake us:
In the great hand of God I stand, and thence
145 Against the undivulged pretence I fight
Of treasonous malice.

MACDUFF: And so do I.

ALL: So all.

MACBETH: Let's briefly put on manly readiness
150 And meet i' the hall together.

their daggers covered with gore. Who could stop himself, if he had a heart to love, and in that heart thecourage to make his love known?

LADY MACBETH: *Help me, please!*

MACDUFF: *Look after the lady.*

MALCOLM: [Aside to Donalbain.] *Why do we not speak, we, who should be doing most of the talking?*

DONALBAIN: [Aside to Malcolm.] *What can be spoken here, where our fate, which is still unclear, could rush in and seize us? Let's leave; our tears are not yet begun.*

MALCOLM: [Aside to Donalbain.] *Nor has our strong sorrow begun to correct this.*

BANQUO: *Look after the lady.*
    [Lady Macbeth is carried out.]
And when we have clothed ourselves properly, let us meet and question this bloody piece of work in order to understand it better. Fears and doubts shake us. In the great hand of God I stand, and I fight against the secret reason for this treason.

MACDUFF: *And so do I.*

ALL: *So all.*

MACBETH: *Let's get dressed quickly and meet together in the great hall.*

ALL: Well contented.

[Exeunt all but Malcolm and Donalbain.]

MALCOLM: What will you do? Let's not consort with them:
To show an unfelt sorrow is an office
Which the false man does easy. I'll to England.

155 DONALBAIN: To Ireland, I; our separated fortune
Shall keep us both the safer. Where we are
There's daggers in men's smiles: the near in blood,
The nearer bloody.

MALCOLM: This murderous shaft that's shot
160 Hath not yet lighted, and our safest way
Is to avoid the aim. Therefore to horse;
And let us not be dainty of leave-taking,
But shift away. There's warrant in that theft
Which steals itself when there's no mercy left.

[Exeunt.]

ALL: Well contented.

> [Exit all but Malcolm and Donalbain.]

MALCOLM: What will you do? Let's not mingle with them. To show a sorrow which is not honestly felt is an easy task for the false man. I'll go to England.

DONALBAIN: I will go to Ireland. By separating we shall keep ourselves safer. Here there are daggers in men's smiles; the nearer in kinship to Duncan, the closer we are to becoming murdered.

MALCOLM: This murderous plot is not yet finished, and our safest plan is to avoid its wrath. Therefore, ride, and let us not be polite in our leaving, but steal away. It is right to run away when there's no mercy left.

> [Exit.]

SCENE 4
Outside Macbeth's castle.

[Enter Ross with an Old Man.]

OLD MAN: Threescore and ten I can remember well:
    Within the volume of which time I have seen
    Hours dreadful and things strange, but this sore night
    Hath trifled former knowings.

5   ROSS: Ah, good father,
    Thou seest the heavens, as troubled with man's act,
    Threaten his bloody stage. By the clock 'tis day,
    And yet dark night strangles the travelling lamp.
    Is't night's predominance, or the day's shame,
10   That darkness does the face of earth entomb,
    When living light should kiss it?

OLD MAN: 'Tis unnatural,
    Even like the deed that's done. On Tuesday last
    A falcon towering in her pride of place
15   Was by a mousing owl hawk'd at and kill'd.

ROSS: And Duncan's horses—a thing most strange and certain—
    Beauteous and swift, the minions of their race,
    Turn'd wild in nature, broke their stalls, flung out,
    Contending 'gainst obedience, as they would make
20   War with mankind.

OLD MAN: 'Tis said they eat each other.

ROSS: They did so, to the amazement of mine eyes
    That look'd upon't.

[Enter Macduff.]

    Here comes the good Macduff.
25   How goes the world, sir, now?

SCENE 4
Outside Macbeth's castle.

[Enter Ross with an Old Man.]

OLD MAN: *I can remember well seventy years, and within that time I have seen many dreadful hours and strange things, but this painful night has trivialized all my previous knowledge.*

ROSS: *Ah, good father, as you see, the heavens are troubled with man's bloody actions. By the clock it should be day, and yet darkness still strangles the sun. Is it night's dominance, or is it the day's shame, that darkness should bury the face of earth at the time when living light should kiss it?*

OLD MAN: *It is unnatural, like the deed that has been done. Last Tuesday a falcon, towering in her majesty, was attacked and killed by a small owl.*

ROSS: *And Duncan's horses—this is a thing most strange—beautiful and swift, prime examples of their race, turned wild and broke their stalls, ran out, and would not be obedient, as if they would war with mankind.*

OLD MAN: *It is said they ate each other.*

ROSS: *They did so, to the amazement of my eyes as I looked upon it.*

[Enter Macduff.]

Here comes the good Macduff. Sir, how goes the world?

MACDUFF: Why, see you not?

ROSS: Is't known who did this more than bloody deed?

MACDUFF: Those that Macbeth hath slain.

ROSS: Alas, the day!
30   What good could they pretend?

MACDUFF: They were suborn'd:
    Malcolm and Donalbain, the King's two sons,
    Are stol'n away and fled, which puts upon them
    Suspicion of the deed.

35   ROSS: 'Gainst nature still!
    Thriftless ambition, that wilt ravin up
    Thine own life's means! Then 'tis most like
    The sovereignty will fall upon Macbeth.

MACDUFF: He is already named, and gone to Scone
40   To be invested.

ROSS: Where is Duncan's body?

MACDUFF: Carried to Colmekill,
    The sacred storehouse of his predecessors
    And guardian of their bones.

45   ROSS: Will you to Scone?

MACDUFF: No, cousin, I'll to Fife.

ROSS: Well, I will thither.

MACDUFF: *Can't you see?*

ROSS: *Is it known yet who killed Duncan?*

MACDUFF: *Those that Macbeth has slain.*

ROSS: *Alas, the day! What profit could they have received from such an act?*

MACDUFF: *They were bribed. Malcolm and Donalbain, the King's two sons, have stolen away, which puts suspicion upon them.*

ROSS: *It is so unnatural! It is absolute ambition to devour one's father! Then it is most likely that Macbeth will be named King.*

MACDUFF: *He is already named; he has gone to Scone to be crowned.*

ROSS: *Where is Duncan's body?*

MACDUFF: *It is carried to Colmekill, the sacred cemetery of his ancestor's bodies, and guardian of their bones.*

ROSS: *Will you to go Scone?*

MACDUFF: *No, cousin, I'll go home.*

ROSS: *Well, I will go there.*

MACDUFF: Well, may you see things well done there, Adieu,
    Lest our old robes sit easier than our new!

50   ROSS: Farewell, father.

OLD MAN: God's benison go with you and with those
    That would make good of bad and friends of foes!

[Exeunt.]

MACDUFF: *Well, may you see things well done there; good-bye. Let's hope that our old clothes don't fit us better than our new ones.*

Ross: *Farewell, father.*

OLD MAN: *God's blessings go with you and with all who would make good of bad and friends of foes!*

[Exit.]

❦

ACT III

SCENE 1
Forres. The palace.

[Enter Banquo.]

BANQUO: Thou hast it now: King, Cawdor, Glamis, all,
    As the weird women promised, and I fear
    Thou play'dst most foully for't: yet it was said
    It should not stand in thy posterity,
5   But that myself should be the root and father
    Of many kings. If there come truth from them—
    As upon thee, Macbeth, their speeches shine—
    Why, by the verities on thee made good,
    May they not be my oracles as well
10   And set me up in hope? But hush, no more.

[Sennet sounded. Enter Macbeth as King, Lady Macbeth as Queen, Lennox, Ross, Lords, Ladies, and Attendants.]

MACBETH: Here's our chief guest.

LADY MACBETH: If he had been forgotten,
    It had been as a gap in our great feast
    And all thing unbecoming.

15   MACBETH: Tonight we hold a solemn supper, sir,
    And I'll request your presence.

ACT III

SCENE 1
Forres. The palace.

[Enter Banquo thinking aloud.]

BANQUO: *Macbeth, you have it now—the titles of King, Cawdor, Glamis, everything the witches promised; and I fear that you did something evil to get it. But it was also said that your title should not be passed to your children, but rather that I should be the root and father of many kings. If further truth comes from the prophecies, as they certainly have come to you, may not these truths be my oracles as well and give me hope? But hush! No more about this.*

[Trumpets sound. Enter Macbeth as King, Lady Macbeth as Queen, Lennox, Ross, Lords, Ladies, and Attendants.]

MACBETH: *Here is our chief guest.*

LADY MACBETH: *If he had been forgotten, there would have been an unbecoming gap in our great feast.*

MACBETH: *Tonight we will hold a stately supper, sir; and I require your presence.*

BANQUO: Let your Highness
    Command upon me, to the which my duties
    Are with a most indissoluble tie
20   Forever knit.

MACBETH: Ride you this afternoon?

BANQUO: Ay, my good lord.

MACBETH: We should have else desired your good advice,
    Which still hath been both grave and prosperous
25   In this day's council; but we'll take tomorrow.
    Is't far you ride?

BANQUO: As far, my lord, as will fill up the time
    'Twixt this and supper. Go not my horse the better,
    I must become a borrower of the night
30   For a dark hour or twain.

MACBETH: Fail not our feast.

BANQUO: My lord, I will not.

MACBETH: We hear our bloody cousins are bestow'd
    In England and in Ireland, not confessing
35   Their cruel parricide, filling their hearers
    With strange invention. But of that tomorrow,
    When therewithal we shall have cause of state
    Craving us jointly. Hie you to horse; adieu,
    Till you return at night. Goes Fleance with you?

40   BANQUO: Ay, my good lord. Our time does call upon's.

MACBETH: I wish your horses swift and sure of foot,
    And so I do commend you to their backs.
    Farewell.   *[Exit Banquo.]*
    Let every man be master of his time
45   Till seven at night; to make society

84

BANQUO: *Let your Highness command me, for my duties are most strongly tied forever to you.*

MACBETH: *Do you ride this afternoon?*

BANQUO: *Yes, my good lord.*

MACBETH: *We should have otherwise desired your good advice, which you have shown so thoughtfully in today's council; but we'll discuss matters tomorrow. Is it far that you ride?*

BANQUO: *As far, my lord, as will fill up our daylight hours. If my horse does not rise to the challenge, I will arrive an hour or two after dark.*

MACBETH: *Do not fail to come to our feast.*

BANQUO: *My lord, I will not.*

MACBETH: *We hear that our bloody cousins, living in England and in Ireland, are not confessing the cruel murder of their father. Instead they tell strange stories. But more of that tomorrow when concerns of the state will require both of us. Go to your horse; good-bye until you return at night. Does Fleance go with you?*

BANQUO: *Yes, my good lord. We need to leave now.*

MACBETH: *I hope your horses are swift and sure of foot, and so I do commend you to their backs. Farewell.*　　　　[Exit Banquo.]
Let every man be master of his own affairs until seven tonight. To prepare for the gathering, we will keep ourselves alone until then.

The sweeter welcome, we will keep ourself
Till supper time alone. While then, God be with you!
                    [Exeunt all but Macbeth and an Attendant.]
Sirrah, a word with you. Attend those men
Our pleasure?

50 ATTENDANT: They are, my lord, without the palace gate.

MACBETH: Bring them before us.   *[Exit Attendant.]*
    To be thus is nothing,
    But to be safely thus. Our fears in Banquo
    Stick deep, and in his royalty of nature
55 Reigns that which would be fear'd. 'Tis much he dares,
    And, to that dauntless temper of his mind,
    He hath a wisdom that doth guide his valor
    To act in safety. There is none but he
    Whose being I do fear; and under him
60 My genius is rebuked, as it is said
    Mark Antony's was by Caesar. He chid the sisters,
    When first they put the name of King upon me,
    And bade them speak to him; then prophet-like
    They hail'd him father to a line of kings:
65 Upon my head they placed a fruitless crown
    And put a barren sceptre in my gripe,
    Thence to be wrench'd with an unlineal hand,
    No son of mine succeeding. If't be so,
    For Banquo's issue have I filed my mind,
70 For them the gracious Duncan have I murdered,
    Put rancors in the vessel of my peace
    Only for them, and mine eternal jewel
    Given to the common enemy of man,
    To make them kings, the seed of Banquo kings!
75 Rather than so, come, Fate, into the list,
    And champion me to the utterance! Who's there?

Well, then, God be with you.
                    [Exit all but Macbeth and an Attendant.]
Sir, a word with you. Do those men wait for us?

ATTENDANT: *Lord, they are outside the palace gate.*

MACBETH: *Bring them here.*   [Exit Attendant.]
To be King is nothing, without being safely King! Our fears about Banquo are deep; and I fear his royal nature is well worth fearing. He dares a lot, and, to that fearless temper of his mind, he adds a wisdom which guides him to act safely. There is no one but he whom I do fear; and because of him, my greatness is stopped, just as Mark Antony's was by Caesar. He scolded the witches when they called me King and asked them to speak to him. Then, like prophets, they hailed him as a father to a line of kings. Upon my head they placed a barren crown and put an empty scepter in my hand, only to be wrenched by someone else's hand, no son of mine will succeed me. If it is so, I defiled my mind for Banquo's heirs; and it is for them that I murdered Duncan and put demons into my peace of mind, only for them. I have given my soul to the devil to make them kings, the sons of Banquo, kings! I would rather battle fate to the death! Who's there?

[Re-enter Attendant, with two Murderers.]

Now go to the door, and stay there till we call.

[Exit Attendant.]

Was it not yesterday we spoke together?

FIRST MURDERER: It was, so please your Highness.

80 MACBETH: Well then, now
　　　Have you consider'd of my speeches? Know
　　　That it was he in the times past which held you
　　　So under fortune, which you thought had been
　　　Our innocent self? This I made good to you
85 　　In our last conference, pass'd in probation with you,
　　　How you were borne in hand, how cross'd, the instruments,
　　　Who wrought with them, and all things else that might
　　　To half a soul and to a notion crazed
　　　Say, "Thus did Banquo."

90 FIRST MURDERER: You made it known to us.

MACBETH: I did so, and went further, which is now
　　　Our point of second meeting. Do you find
　　　Your patience so predominant in your nature,
　　　That you can let this go? Are you so gospell'd,
95 　　To pray for this good man and for his issue,
　　　Whose heavy hand hath bow'd you to the grave
　　　And beggar'd yours for ever?

FIRST MURDERER: We are men, my liege.

MACBETH: Ay, in the catalogue ye go for men,
100 　　As hounds and greyhounds, mongrels, spaniels, curs,
　　　Shoughs, waterrugs, and demi-wolves are clept
　　　All by the name of dogs. The valued file
　　　Distinguishes the swift, the slow, the subtle,
　　　The housekeeper, the hunter, every one
105 　　According to the gift which bounteous nature

[Re-enter Attendant, with two Murderers.]

Go to the door, and stay there until we call you.
                                        [Exit Attendant.]
It was yesterday, was it not, when we spoke together?

FIRST MURDERER: *It was, so please your Highness.*

MACBETH: *Have you now thought about what I said? You now know that it was Banquo in times past who held you in misfortune, while you thought it had been me. This I made clear to you in our last conference; I gave you proof of how you were mishandled, how deceived, what instruments were used and who manipulated them, and everything else that might confirm to a crazed soul that "Thus did Banquo."*

FIRST MURDERER: *You made it known to us.*

MACBETH: *I and went even further, which is why we are having a second meeting. Do you find yourself so patient that you can forget past injuries? Are you so religious to pray for this good man and his children when his heavy hand has bowed you to the grave and made your families so poor?*

FIRST MURDERER: *We are men, my lord.*

MACBETH: *Yes, in the catalogue you go for men; just as hounds and grey-hounds, mongrels, spaniels, curs, shoughs, water-dogs, and half-wolves are called all by the name of dog. A better listing distinguishes the swift, the slow, the subtle, the housekeeper, the hunter, every one according to the gift which nature has given him, separating each with specific qualities. And so are men. If you should be placed anywhere in the file as something other*

Hath in him closed, whereby he does receive
Particular addition, from the bill
That writes them all alike; and so of men.
Now if you have a station in the file,
110 Not i' the worst rank of manhood, say it,
And I will put that business in your bosoms
Whose execution takes your enemy off,
Grapples you to the heart and love of us,
Who wear our health but sickly in his life,
115 Which in his death were perfect.

SECOND MURDERER: I am one, my liege,
Whom the vile blows and buffets of the world
Have so incensed that I am reckless what
I do to spite the world.

120 FIRST MURDERER: And I another
So weary with disasters, tugg'd with fortune,
That I would set my life on any chance,
To mend it or be rid on 't.

MACBETH: Both of you
125 Know Banquo was your enemy.

BOTH MURDERERS: True, my lord.

MACBETH: So is he mine, and in such bloody distance
That every minute of his being thrusts
Against my near'st of life: and though I could
130 With barefaced power sweep him from my sight
And bid my will avouch it, yet I must not,
For certain friends that are both his and mine,
Whose loves I may not drop, but wail his fall
Who I myself struck down. And thence it is
135 That I to your assistance do make love,
Masking the business from the common eye
For sundry weighty reasons.

than the worst rank of man, say it; for I will give you a job whose execution will eliminate your enemy and win you into my friendship, since we have a mutual enemy whose death will make us whole again.

SECOND MURDERER: *I am one, my lord, who the vile blows and buffets of the world have so angered that I don't cae what i have to do to spite the world.*

FIRST MURDERER: *And I another so weary with disasters, so beaten by life's troubles, that I would set my life on any chance to mend it or be rid of it.*

MACBETH: *Both of you know Banquo is your enemy.*

BOTH MURDERERS: *Yes, my lord.*

MACBETH: *He is also mine; and an enemy in such a bloody manner that every minute that he lives, he threatens my life. Though I have the power to sweep him from my sight and justify it, yet I must not do so. I need certain friends who are both his and mine, so I must lament the death of him whom I would, myself, strike down. Therefore, I need your assistance masking this business from the public eye for various weighty reasons.*

SECOND MURDERER: We shall, my lord,
    Perform what you command us.

140   FIRST MURDERER: Though our lives—

MACBETH: Your spirits shine through you. Within this hour at most
    I will advise you where to plant yourselves,
    Acquaint you with the perfect spy o' the time,
    The moment on 't; for 't must be done tonight,
145   And something from the palace; always thought
    That I require a clearness; and with him—
    To leave no rubs nor botches in the work—
    Fleance his son, that keeps him company,
    Whose absence is no less material to me
150   Than is his father's, must embrace the fate
    Of that dark hour. Resolve yourselves apart:
    I'll come to you anon.

BOTH MURDERERS: We are resolved, my lord.

MACBETH: I'll call upon you straight. Abide within.
                    [Exeunt murderers.]
155   It is concluded: Banquo, thy soul's flight,
    If it find heaven, must find it out tonight.

                            [Exit.]

SECOND MURDERER: *We shall, my lord, perform what you command us.*

FIRST MURDERER: *Though our lives—*

MACBETH: *Your true spirits shine through you. Within this hour at most, I will advise you where to place yourselves, acquaint you with the perfect report of the time, and the moment in which to do it. For it must be done tonight. And do it at some distance from the palace since I need to be above suspicion. And in addition to him, to leave no loose ends, Fleance his son, who keeps him company—and whose absence is no less important to me than is his father's—must also die. Make up your minds; I'll come to you shortly.*

BOTH MURDERERS: *We are ready, my lord.*

MACBETH: *I'll call upon you straight away; stay inside.*
                                        [Exit Murders.]
It is concluded Banquo, the flight of your soul, if it is to find heaven, must find it out tonight.

                                        [Exit.]

SCENE 2
The palace.

[Enter Lady Macbeth and a Servant.]

LADY MACBETH: Is Banquo gone from court?

SERVANT: Ay, madam, but returns again tonight.

LADY MACBETH: Say to the King I would attend his leisure
    For a few words.

5   SERVANT: Madam, I will.   *[Exit.]*

LADY MACBETH: Nought's had, all's spent,
    Where our desire is got without content.
    'Tis safer to be that which we destroy
    Than by destruction dwell in doubtful joy.

[Enter Macbeth.]

10   How now, my lord! Why do you keep alone,
    Of sorriest fancies your companions making,
    Using those thoughts which should indeed have died
    With them they think on? Things without all remedy
    Should be without regard. What's done is done.

15   MACBETH: We have scotch'd the snake, not kill'd it.
    She'll close and be herself, whilst our poor malice
    Remains in danger of her former tooth.
    But let the frame of things disjoint, both the worlds suffer,
    Ere we will eat our meal in fear and sleep
20   In the affliction of these terrible dreams
    That shake us nightly. Better be with the dead,
    Whom we, to gain our peace, have sent to peace,
    Than on the torture of the mind to lie
    In restless ecstasy. Duncan is in his grave;

SCENE 2
The palace.

[Enter Lady Macbeth and a Servant.]

LADY MACBETH: *Has Banquo left the court?*

SERVANT: *Yes, madam, but he returns again tonight.*

LADY MACBETH: *Say to the King that I wish to speak a few words with him.*

SERVANT: *Madam, I will.*   [Exit.]

LADY MACBETH: *All our efforts have been wasted if we can't be content in our new life. It is safer to be Duncan than to dwell in such apprehension.*

[Enter Macbeth.]

What, my lord! Why do you keep by yourself, making strange fantasies your companions and thinking those thoughts which should have died with Duncan? Things without a cure should not be thought upon. What's done is done.

MACBETH: *We have cut the snake, not killed it; she'll heal and be whole while our feeble attempt remains in danger of revenge. But let the universe fall apart, both heaven and earth suffer, before we will eat our meals in fear and sleep in the nightmares which shake us nightly. It is better to be with the dead, whom we have sent to peace to gain our peace, rather than lie here in wretched agony. Duncan is in his grave; he sleeps well after life's fitful fever. Treason has done his worst. No knife, poison, civil war, - foreign invasion, nothing, can touch him any further.*

95

25   After life's fitful fever he sleeps well;
    Treason has done his worst: nor steel, nor poison,
    Malice domestic, foreign levy, nothing,
    Can touch him further.

LADY MACBETH: Come on,
30   Gentle my lord, sleek o'er your rugged looks;
    Be bright and jovial among your guests tonight.

MACBETH: So shall I, love, and so, I pray, be you:
    Let your remembrance apply to Banquo;
    Present him eminence, both with eye and tongue:
35   Unsafe the while, that we
    Must lave our honors in these flattering streams,
    And make our faces vizards to our hearts,
    Disguising what they are.

LADY MACBETH: You must leave this.

40 MACBETH: O, full of scorpions is my mind, dear wife!
    Thou know'st that Banquo and his Fleance lives.

LADY MACBETH: But in them nature's copy's not eterne.

MACBETH: There's comfort yet; they are assailable.
    Then be thou jocund. Ere the bat hath flown
45   His cloister'd flight; ere to black Hecate's summons
    The shard-borne beetle with his drowsy hums
    Hath rung night's yawning peal, there shall be done
    A deed of dreadful note.

LADY MACBETH: What's to be done?

50 MACBETH: Be innocent of the knowledge, dearest chuck,
    Till thou applaud the deed. Come, seeling night,
    Scarf up the tender eye of pitiful day,
    And with thy bloody and invisible hand
    Cancel and tear to pieces that great bond

LADY MACBETH: *Come on, easy my lord, cover over your rough looks; be bright and happy among your guests tonight.*

MACBETH: *So I shall, love, and so, I pray, you shall also. Remember to talk of Banquo; give him praise with both eye and tongue. Since we may be unsafe, we must cleanse our honors in these flattering streams and make our faces masks to our hearts, disguising what they really feel.*

LADY MACBETH: *You must leave this.*

MACBETH: *O, my mind is full of scorpions, dear wife! You know that Banquo and his Fleance live.*

LADY MACBETH: *But they won't live forever.*

MACBETH: *There's comfort in that; they are attackable. Be happy. Before the bat has flown tonight, before the dung beetle with his drowsy hums has completed the night's song as Hecate bids, there will be done a deed of most dreadful note.*

LADY MACBETH: *What's to be done?*

MACBETH: *Be innocent of the knowledge, my dear one, until you can applaud the deed. Come, dark night, seal up the tender eye of pitiful day; and with your bloody and invisible hand cancel and tear to pieces Banquo's life, which still frightens me! Light diminishes, and the crow returns to her nest. The good things of day*

55 Which keeps me pale! Light thickens, and the crow
Makes wing to the rooky wood:
Good things of day begin to droop and drowse,
Whiles night's black agents to their preys do rouse.
Thou marvell'st at my words, but hold thee still:
Things bad begun make strong themselves by ill.
So, prithee, go with me.

[Exeunt.]

SCENE 3
A park near the palace.

[Enter three Murderers.]

FIRST MURDERER: But who did bid thee join with us?

THIRD MURDERER: Macbeth.

SECOND MURDERER: He needs not our mistrust, since he delivers
Our offices and what we have to do,
5 To the direction just.

FIRST MURDERER: Then stand with us.
The west yet glimmers with some streaks of day;
Now spurs the lated traveller apace
To gain the timely inn, and near approaches
10 The subject of our watch.

THIRD MURDERER: Hark! I hear horses.

BANQUO: *[Within.]* Give us a light there, ho!

SECOND MURDERER: Then 'tis he: the rest
That are within the note of expectation
15 Already are i' the court.

begin to grow sleepy while night's black agents are roused to seek their prey. You are shocked at my words; but hold still now, for things that start out bad make themselves strong by more evil. So, I pray you, go with me.

[Exit.]

SCENE 3

A park near the palace.

[Enter three Murderers.]

FIRST MURDERER: *But who bid you to join with us?*

THIRD MURDERER: *Macbeth.*

SECOND MURDERER: *He does not need our mistrust since he delivers our instructions.*

FIRST MURDERER: *Then stand with us. The western sky yet shows some streaks of day; the approaching darkness speeds the late traveler to reach the castle quickly; and here comes the subject of our watch.*

THIRD MURDERER: *Listen! I hear horses.*

BANQUO: [Within.] *Give us a light there, now!*

SECOND MURDERER: *Then it is Banquo; the rest of the expected guests already are in the court.*

ACT III SCENE 3

FIRST MURDERER: His horses go about.

THIRD MURDERER: Almost a mile, but he does usually—
So all men do—from hence to the palace gate
Make it their walk.

20   SECOND MURDERER: A light, a light!

[Enter Banquo, and Fleance with a torch.]

THIRD MURDERER: 'Tis he.

FIRST MURDERER: Stand to't.

BANQUO: It will be rain tonight.

FIRST MURDERER: Let it come down.
                     [They set upon Banquo.]

25   BANQUO: O, treachery! Fly, good Fleance, fly, fly, fly!
Thou mayst revenge. O slave!
        [Dies. Fleance escapes.]

THIRD MURDERER: Who did strike out the light?

FIRST MURDERER: Was't not the way?

30   THIRD MURDERER: There's but one down; the son is fled.

SECOND MURDERER: We have lost
Best half of our affair.

FIRST MURDERER: Well, let's away and say how much is done.

                            [Exeunt.]

FIRST MURDERER: *His horses go about.*

THIRD MURDERER: *Yes, almost a mile, but he usually does. All men walk the distance from here to the palace gate.*

SECOND MURDERER: *A light, a light approaches!*

[Enter Banquo and Fleance with a torch.]

THIRD MURDERER: *It is he.*

FIRST MURDERER: *Stand ready.*

BANQUO: *It will rain tonight.*

FIRST MURDERER: *Let it come down.*
[They set upon Banquo.]

BANQUO: *O, treachery! Run, good Fleance. Fly, fly, fly! Revenge this. O, slave!*
[Banquo dies, Fleance escapes.]

THIRD MURDERER: *Who struck out the light?*

FIRST MURDERER: *Wasn't that what we agreed?*

THIRD MURDERER: *There is only but one killed; the son has fled.*

SECOND MURDERER: *We have lost the better half of our affair.*

FIRST MURDERER: *Well, let's leave and report what has been done.*

[Exit.]

SCENE 4
A hall in the palace.

[A banquet prepared. Enter Macbeth, Lady Macbeth, Ross, Lennox, Lords, and Attendants.]

MACBETH: You know your own degrees; sit down. At first
  And last the hearty welcome.

LORDS: Thanks to your Majesty.

MACBETH: Ourself will mingle with society
5   And play the humble host.
  Our hostess keeps her state, but in best time
  We will require her welcome.

LADY MACBETH: Pronounce it for me, sir, to all our friends,
  For my heart speaks they are welcome.

[Enter first Murderer to the door.]

10   MACBETH: See, they encounter thee with their hearts' thanks.
  Both sides are even: here I'll sit i' the midst:
  Be large in mirth; anon we'll drink a measure
  The table round. *[Approaches the door.]*
  There's blood upon thy face.

15   MURDERER: 'Tis Banquo's then.

MACBETH: 'Tis better thee without than he within.
  Is he dispatch'd?

MURDERER: My lord, his throat is cut; that I did for him.

20   MACBETH: Thou art the best o' the cut-throats! Yet he's good
  That did the like for Fleance. If thou didst it,
  Thou art the nonpareil.

SCENE 4

A hall in the palace.

[A banquet prepared. Enter Macbeth, Lady Macbeth, Ross, Lennox, Lords, and Attendants.]

MACBETH: *You know your own ranks; sit down. At first and last we welcome you all.*

LORDS: *Thanks to your Majesty.*

MACBETH: *I will mingle with society and play the humble host. Our hostess keeps her seat, but shortly we will ask her to give you all a welcome.*

LADY MACBETH: *Say it for me, sir, to all our friends; for my heart speaks that they are welcome.*

[Enter first Murderer to the door.]

MACBETH: [To Lady Macbeth.] *See, they return their heartfelt thanks to you. Both sides are even.* [Putting his hand on an empty chair.] *Here I'll sit in the middle.* [Walks to the door.] *Be full of joy; let's drink a toast to the whole table.* [Aside at door.] *There's blood on your face.*

MURDERER: *It is Banquo's then.*

MACBETH: *It is better you have his blood on you than he has it inside his body. Is he dead?*

MURDERER: *My lord, I cut his throat for him.*

MACBETH: *You are the best of the cutthroats; yet he is also good who did the same for Fleance. If you did it, you are unequalled.*

MURDERER: Most royal sir,
Fleance is 'scaped.

MACBETH: *[Aside.]* Then comes my fit again: I had else been perfect,
25   Whole as the marble, founded as the rock,
As broad and general as the casing air:
But now I am cabin'd, cribb'd, confined, bound in
To saucy doubts and fears.—But Banquo's safe?

MURDERER: Ay, my good lord. Safe in a ditch he bides,
30   With twenty trenched gashes on his head;
The least a death to nature.

MACBETH: Thanks for that.
There the grown serpent lies; the worm that's fled
Hath nature that in time will venom breed,
35   No teeth for the present. Get thee gone. Tomorrow
We'll hear ourselves again.

[Exit Murderer.]

LADY MACBETH: My royal lord,
You do not give the cheer. The feast is sold
That is not often vouch'd, while 'tis a-making,
40   'Tis given with welcome. To feed were best at home;
From thence the sauce to meat is ceremony;
Meeting were bare without it.

MACBETH: Sweet remembrancer!
Now good digestion wait on appetite,
45   And health on both!

LENNOX: May't please your Highness sit.

[The Ghost of Banquo enters and sits in Macbeth's place.]

MACBETH: Here had we now our country's honor roof'd,
Were the graced person of our Banquo present;
Who may I rather challenge for unkindness
50   Than pity for mischance!

MURDERER: *Most royal sir, Fleance has escaped.*

MACBETH: [Aside.] *Then my fit comes again; I otherwise would have been perfect, stable as a foundation made of rocks, as broad and general as the coverings are. But now I am cabined, controlled, confined, bound up with strange doubts and fears. But Banquo's dead?*

MURDERER: *Yes, my good lord; he rests safe in a ditch with twenty deep gashes on his head, any one of which would have killed me.*

MACBETH: *Thanks for that. There the grown serpent lies. The worm has fled. Fleance has a nature that in time will breed poison, but he has no teeth for the present. Get out. Tomorrow we'll talk again.*

[Exit Murderer.]

LADY MACBETH: *My royal lord, you do not give the toast; our meeting is bare without a proper toast to assure guests of their welcome. We need ceremony if we are not to feel we are at an inn or at home.*

MACBETH: *Sweet reminder! Health and good digestion wait on you all.*

LENNOX: *May it please your Highness, sit.*

[The Ghost of Banquo enters and sits in Macbeth's place.]

MACBETH: *Here we would now have all our country's honored men, if Banquo were present; I question his lack of kindness rather than hope he has had a mishap.*

ROSS: His absence, sir,
    Lays blame upon his promise. Please't your Highness
    To grace us with your royal company?

MACBETH: The table's full.

55   LENNOX: Here is a place reserved, sir.

MACBETH: Where?

LENNOX: Here, my good lord. What is't that moves your Highness?

MACBETH: Which of you have done this?

LORDS: What, my good lord?

60   MACBETH: Thou canst not say I did it: never shake
    Thy gory locks at me.

ROSS: Gentlemen, rise; his Highness is not well.

LADY MACBETH: Sit, worthy friends; my lord is often thus,
    And hath been from his youth. Pray you, keep seat.
    The fit is momentary; upon a thought
65   He will again be well. If much you note him,
    You shall offend him and extend his passion:
    Feed, and regard him not. Are you a man?

MACBETH: Ay, and a bold one, that dare look on that
    Which might appal the devil.

70   LADY MACBETH: O proper stuff!
    This is the very painting of your fear;
    This is the air-drawn dagger which, you said,
    Led you to Duncan. O, these flaws and starts,
    Impostors to true fear, would well become
75   A woman's story at a winter's fire,

ROSS: *His absence, sir, lays blame upon his promise. Please grace us with your royal company, your Highness.*

MACBETH: *The table's full.*

LENNOX: *Here is a place reserved for you, sir.*

MACBETH: *Where?*

LENNOX: *Here, my good lord. What is it that startles your Highness?*

MACBETH: *Which of you have done this?*

LORDS: *What is it, lord?*

MACBETH: [Staring at Banquo's ghost.] *You can not say I did it; do not shake your gory locks at me.*

ROSS: *Gentlemen, rise; his Highness is not well.*

LADY MACBETH: *Sit, worthy friends. My lord is often like this and has been since his youth. Please sit; this fit is momentary. In just a moment he will be well again. If you notice him too much, you shall offend him and extend his attack. Eat, and do not look at him.* [Aside to Macbeth.] *Are you a man?*

MACBETH: *Yes, and a bold one that dares look on that which might appall the devil.*

LADY MACBETH: *O, this is fine. This is the very painting of your fear; this is the same as the dagger which led you to Duncan. These imaginary fits and starts, imitations of true fear, would become a woman's story in front of a winter's fire, written by her*

Authorized by her grandam. Shame itself!
Why do you make such faces? When all's done,
You look but on a stool.

MACBETH: Prithee, see there! Behold! Look! Lo! How say you?
80   Why, what care I? If thou canst nod, speak too.
If charnel houses and our graves must send
Those that we bury back, our monuments
Shall be the maws of kites.

[Exit Ghost.]

LADY MACBETH: What, quite unmann'd in folly?

85   MACBETH: If I stand here, I saw him.

LADY MACBETH: Fie, for shame!

MACBETH: Blood hath been shed ere now, i' the olden time,
Ere humane statute purged the gentle weal;
Ay, and since too, murders have been perform'd
90   Too terrible for the ear. The time has been,
That, when the brains were out, the man would die,
And there an end; but now they rise again,
With twenty mortal murders on their crowns,
And push us from our stools. This is more strange
95   Than such a murder is.

LADY MACBETH: My worthy lord,
Your noble friends do lack you.

MACBETH: I do forget.
Do not muse at me, my most worthy friends.
100   I have a strange infirmity, which is nothing
To those that know me. Come, love and health to all;
Then I'll sit down. Give me some wine, fill full.
I drink to the general joy o' the whole table,
And to our dear friend Banquo, whom we miss.
105   Would he were here! To all and him we thirst,
And all to all.

grandmother. Shame on you! Why do you make such faces? When all is said and done, you look only on a chair.

MACBETH: *See there! Behold! Look! What do you say now? Why, what do I care? If you can nod your head, speak, too. If graves send back those we bury, our monuments shall be the stomachs of birds.*

[Exit Ghost.]

LADY MACBETH: *What, are you crazy?*

MACBETH: *As I stand here, I saw him.*

LADY MACBETH: *Ha, for shame!*

MACBETH: *Blood has been shed before now, in the olden days before laws purged the society. Yes, and since then murders have been performed that are too terrible for the ear. There was a time, when once the brains were out of the skull, a man would die, and that was the end. Now they rise again, with twenty fatal wounds on their heads, and push us from our seats. This is more strange than such a murder is.*

LADY MACBETH: *My worthy lord, your noble friends are waiting for you.*

MACBETH: *I do forget. Most worthy friends, do not worry about me. I have a strange illness, which is nothing to those that know me. Come, love and health to all; then I'll sit down. Give me some wine; fill the goblet full. I drink to the general joy of all at the table and to our dear friend Banquo, whom we dearly miss. I wish he were here! To all, and to him, we drink.*

LORDS: Our duties and the pledge.

[Re-enter Ghost.]

MACBETH: Avaunt, and quit my sight! Let the earth hide thee!
    Thy bones are marrowless, thy blood is cold;
110   Thou hast no speculation in those eyes
    Which thou dost glare with.

LADY MACBETH: Think of this, good peers,
    But as a thing of custom. 'Tis no other,
    Only it spoils the pleasure of the time.

115   MACBETH: What man dare, I dare.
    Approach thou like the rugged Russian bear,
    The arm'd rhinoceros, or the Hyrcan tiger;
    Take any shape but that, and my firm nerves
    Shall never tremble. Or be alive again,
120   And dare me to the desert with thy sword.
    If trembling I inhabit then, protest me
    The baby of a girl. Hence, horrible shadow!
    Unreal mockery, hence!   *[Exit Ghost.]*
    Why, so: being gone,
125   I am a man again. Pray you, sit still.

LADY MACBETH: You have displaced the mirth, broke the good
                meeting,
    With most admired disorder.

MACBETH: Can such things be,
    And overcome us like a summer's cloud,
130   Without our special wonder? You make me strange
    Even to the disposition that I owe,
    When now I think you can behold such sights,
    And keep the natural ruby of your cheeks
    When mine is blanch'd with fear.

LORDS: *Our duties and the pledge.*

[Re-enter ghost.]

MACBETH: *Leave, and quit my sight! Let the earth hide you! Your bones are marrowless, your blood is cold; you have no life in those eyes with which you glare.*

LADY MACBETH: *Think of this, good friends, as only a customary thing; it is of no consequence, except that it spoils the pleasure of this time.*

MACBETH: [To the ghost.] *What men dare, I dare. If you took the form of the rugged Russian bear, the horned rhinoceros, or the Hyrcan tiger, any shape but this, then my firm nerves would never tremble. Or be alive again and with your sword dare me to go to the desert. If I tremble, tell everyone that I am a puny little child. Away, horrible shadow! Unreal image, away!* [Exit ghost.] *Why, so, with it being gone, I am a man again. Please, sit still.*

LADY MACBETH: *You have dispelled the happiness, and broken our good meeting with this most strange disorder.*

MACBETH: *Can such things be viewed and overtake us like a summer's cloud without our special wonder? You make me wonder at my own disposition. You can behold such sights and keep the natural color of your cheeks, when mine are white with fear.*

135   ROSS: What sights, my lord?

LADY MACBETH: I pray you, speak not; he grows worse and worse;
    Question enrages him. At once, good night:
    Stand not upon the order of your going,
    But go at once.

140   LENNOX: Good night, and better health
    Attend his Majesty!

LADY MACBETH: A kind good night to all!

[Exeunt all but Macbeth and Lady Macbeth.]

MACBETH: It will have blood: they say blood will have blood.
    Stones have been known to move and trees to speak;
145   Augures and understood relations have
    By maggot pies and choughs and rooks brought forth
    The secret'st man of blood. What is the night?

LADY MACBETH: Almost at odds with morning, which is which.

MACBETH: How say'st thou, that Macduff denies his person
150   At our great bidding?

LADY MACBETH: Did you send to him, sir?

MACBETH: I hear it by the way, but I will send.
    There's not a one of them but in his house
    I keep a servant fee'd. I will tomorrow,
155   And betimes I will, to the weird sisters.
    More shall they speak; for now I am bent to know,
    By the worst means, the worst. For mine own good
    All causes shall give way. I am in blood
    Stepp'd in so far that, should I wade no more,
160   Returning were as tedious as go o'er.
    Strange things I have in head that will to hand,
    Which must be acted ere they may be scann'd.

ROSS: *What sights, my lord?*

LADY MACBETH: *I pray you, do not speak; he grows worse and worse. Questions enrage him. At once, good night; do not stand on formalities, but go at once.*

LENNOX: *Good night, and better health to his Majesty!*

LADY MACBETH: *A kind good-night to all!*

[Exit all but Macbeth and Lady Macbeth.]

MACBETH: *It will have blood: they say blood will have more blood. Stones have been known to move and trees to speak; omens and sorcery have uncovered murderers using magpies and crows and rooks. What time is it?*

LADY MACBETH: *It's almost dawn.*

MACBETH: *What do you say to the fact that Macduff does not come at our great bidding?*

LADY MACBETH: *Did you send for him, sir?*

MACBETH: *I hear it by the way, but I will send for him. There's not a single lord in whose house I do not keep a spy. I will go early tomorrow to the witches. More shall they speak to me, for now I am bent to know the worst news from this worst of sources. For my own good, all causes shall give way. I have stepped so far in blood, it is as easy to go forward as it would be to turn back. I have strange things in my head which will be acted upon before I look on them.*

LADY MACBETH: You lack the season of all natures, sleep.

MACBETH: Come, we'll to sleep. My strange and self-abuse
165   Is the initiate fear that wants hard use.
We are yet but young in deed.

[Exeunt.]

SCENE 5
A heath.

[Thunder. Enter the three Witches, meeting Hecate.]

FIRST WITCH: Why, how now, Hecate? You look angerly.

HECATE: Have I not reason, beldams as you are,
Saucy and overbold? How did you dare
To trade and traffic with Macbeth
5   In riddles and affairs of death;
And I, the mistress of your charms,
The close contriver of all harms,
Was never call'd to bear my part,
Or show the glory of our art?
10   And, which is worse, all you have done
Hath been but for a wayward son,
Spiteful and wrathful: who, as others do,
Loves for his own ends, not for you.
But make amends now. Get you gone,
15   And at the pit of Acheron
Meet me i' the morning. Thither he
Will come to know his destiny.
Your vessels and your spells provide,
Your charms and every thing beside.
20   I am for the air; this night I'll spend
Unto a dismal and a fatal end.

LADY MACBETH: *You are overly tired, my lord.*

MACBETH: *Come, we'll go to sleep. My strange self-abuse is only the fear of a novice who is unpracticed in such deeds.*

[Exit.]

SCENE 5
A heath.

[Thunder. Enter the three Witches, meeting Hecate.]

FIRST WITCH: *Why, Hecate! You look angry.*

HECATE: *I have reason, you overly bold hags. How did you dare trade and traffic with Macbeth in riddles and affairs of death while I, the mistress of your spells and the maker of your powers, was never called to bear my part or show what we are capable of doing? And, which is worse, all you have accomplished has been only for a wayward son, spiteful and wrathful, who, as others do, loves only for his own gains, not for your dark powers. But you may make amends now. Leave, and at the pit of Acheron meet me in the morning. There will Macbeth come to know his destiny. Provide him with your vessels and your spells, your charms, and everything else. I will fly; I'll spend this night working for a*

Great business must be wrought ere noon:
Upon the corner of the moon
There hangs a vaporous drop profound;
25   I'll catch it ere it come to ground.
And that distill'd by magic sleights
Shall raise such artificial sprites
As by the strength of their illusion
Shall draw him on to his confusion.
30   He shall spurn fate, scorn death, and bear
His hopes 'bove wisdom, grace, and fear.
And you all know security
Is mortals' chiefest enemy.
            [Music and a song within, "Come away, come away."]
Hark! I am call'd; my little spirit, see,
35   Sits in a foggy cloud and stays for me.

[Exit.]

FIRST WITCH: Come, let's make haste; she'll soon be back again.

[Exeunt.]

dismal and a fatal end. Great business must be completed before mid-day. Upon the corner of the moon, there hangs a low-hanging vaporous drop which I'll catch before it comes to the ground. That, distilled by magical means, shall raise such artificial spirits that the strength of their illusion shall draw him on to his destruction. He shall spurn fate, and scorn death. He shall let his hopes rise above wisdom, fear, and grace; and you all know over-confidence is man's chief enemy.

[Music and a song within, "Come away, come away."]
Listen! I am called; my little spirit sits in a foggy cloud and stays just for me.

[Exit.]

FIRST WITCH: Come, let's hurry; she'll soon be back again.

[Exit.]

SCENE 6
Forres. The palace.

[Enter Lennox and another Lord.]

LENNOX: My former speeches have but hit your thoughts,
    Which can interpret farther: only I say
    Things have been strangely borne. The gracious Duncan
    Was pitied of Macbeth: marry, he was dead.
5   And the right valiant Banquo walk'd too late,
    Whom, you may say, if't please you, Fleance kill'd,
    For Fleance fled. Men must not walk too late.
    Who cannot want the thought, how monstrous
    It was for Malcolm and for Donalbain
10   To kill their gracious father? Damned fact!
    How it did grieve Macbeth! Did he not straight,
    In pious rage, the two delinquents tear,
    That were the slaves of drink and thralls of sleep?
    Was not that nobly done? Ay, and wisely too,
15   For 'twould have anger'd any heart alive
    To hear the men deny't. So that, I say,
    He has borne all things well; and I do think
    That, had he Duncan's sons under his key—
    As, an't please heaven, he shall not—they should find
20   What 'twere to kill a father; so should Fleance.
    But, peace! For from broad words, and 'cause he fail'd
    His presence at the tyrant's feast, I hear,
    Macduff lives in disgrace. Sir, can you tell
    Where he bestows himself?

25 LORD: The son of Duncan,
    From whom this tyrant holds the due of birth,
    Lives in the English court and is received
    Of the most pious Edward with such grace
    That the malevolence of fortune nothing
30   Takes from his high respect. Thither Macduff
    Is gone to pray the holy King, upon his aid
    To wake Northumberland and warlike Siward;

SCENE 6

Forres. The palace.

[Enter Lennox and another Lord.]

LENNOX: *My former words have but confirmed your thoughts, which can be interpreted farther. Only this I say: things have been strangely carried. The gracious Duncan was pitied by Macbeth; soon, he was dead. And the valiant Banquo walked too late; whom, you may say, if it please you, that Fleance killed, for Fleance has fled. Men must not walk too late. Who cannot help thinking how monstrous it was for Malcolm and for Donalbain to kill their gracious father? Damned fact! How it did grieve Macbeth! Did he not immediately, in pious rage, kill the two offenders, that were the slaves of drink and servants of sleep? Was that not nobly done? Yes, and it was wise too, for it would have angered any heart alive to hear these men deny the murder. So I say, he has borne all things well, and I do think that if he had Duncan's sons under his protection—as, if it please heaven, he does not—they would find out what the price is for killing a father. So should Fleance. But, peace! Because he was outspoken and because he didn't come to the tyrant's feast, I hear that Macduff lives in disgrace. Sir, can you tell where he has gone?*

LORD: *The son of Duncan, from whom the tyrannous Macbeth withholds the crown, lives in the English court and is received by the most pious King Edward with such style that his bad fortune does not detract from the respect he is given. Macduff has gone to ask the holy King, on behalf of Malcolm, to stir the northern people and warlike Siward. With their help—and with God's help to justify the work—we may again hold feasts, sleep at night, and*

That by the help of these, with Him above
To ratify the work, we may again
35   Give to our tables meat, sleep to our nights,
Free from our feasts and banquets bloody knives,
Do faithful homage, and receive free honors—
All which we pine for now. And this report
Hath so exasperate the King that he
40   Prepares for some attempt of war.

LENNOX: Sent he to Macduff?

LORD: He did: and with an absolute "Sir, not I,"
The cloudy messenger turns me his back,
And hums, as who should say, "You'll rue the time
45   That clogs me with this answer."

LENNOX: And that well might
Advise him to a caution, to hold what distance
His wisdom can provide. Some holy angel
Fly to the court of England and unfold
50   His message ere he come, that a swift blessing
May soon return to this our suffering country
Under a hand accursed!

LORD: I'll send my prayers with him.

[Exeunt.]

not fear for our lives; we may again do our faithful homage and receive deserved honors. All of this we pine for now; and this report has so incensed Macbeth that he prepares for some attempt of war.

LENNOX: *Did he send for Macduff?*

LORD: *He did, and Macduff said absolutely "not." The distraught messenger turns his back on him and hums, as if saying, "You'll regret giving me that answer."*

LENNOX: *And that well might warn Macduff to keep at a greater distance. If only some holy angel could fly to the court of England and unfold this message before Macduff gets there. Then a swift blessing might soon return to this our country, suffering under the accursed hand of Macbeth!*

LORD: *I'll send my prayers with him.*

[Exit.]

ACT IV

SCENE 1
A cavern. In the middle, a boiling cauldron.

[Thunder. Enter the three Witches.]

FIRST WITCH: Thrice the brinded cat hath mew'd.

SECOND WITCH: Thrice and once the hedge-pig whined.

THIRD WITCH: Harpier cries, "'Tis time, 'tis time."

FIRST WITCH: Round about the cauldron go:
5   In the poison'd entrails throw.
Toad, that under cold stone
Days and nights has thirty-one
Swelter'd venom sleeping got,
Boil thou first i' the charmed pot.

10 ALL: Double, double, toil and trouble;
Fire burn and cauldron bubble.

SECOND WITCH: Fillet of a fenny snake,
In the cauldron boil and bake;
Eye of newt and toe of frog,
15   Wool of bat and tongue of dog,
Adder's fork and blind-worm's sting,
Lizard's leg and howlet's wing,
For a charm of powerful trouble,
Like a hell-broth boil and bubble.

ACT IV

SCENE 1

A cavern. In the middle, a boiling cauldron.

[Thunder. Enter the three Witches.]

FIRST WITCH: *Three times the spotted cat has mewed.*

SECOND WITCH: *Three times, and once the hedgehog has whined.*

THIRD WITCH: *Harpier cries, "It is time, it is time."*

FIRST WITCH: *Go round about this kettle.   Throw into it the poisoned intestines of a toad that under a cold stone has been sleeping for thirty-one days to strengthen its venom. Boil it first in the charmed kettle.*

ALL: *Double, double, toil and trouble; fire burn and cauldron bubble.*

SECOND WITCH: *Put a fillet of a snake from the swamp into the pot and boil and bake it. Eye of newt and toe of frog, fur of bat and tongue of dog, snake's forked tongue, and a blind-worm's sting, lizard's leg and little owl's wing: for a charm of trouble that is powerful, like a hell-broth boil and bubble.*

20 ALL: Double, double, toil and trouble;
    Fire burn and cauldron bubble.

THIRD WITCH: Scale of dragon, tooth of wolf,
    Witch's mummy, maw and gulf
    Of the ravin'd salt-sea shark,
25   Root of hemlock digg'd i' the dark,
    Liver of blaspheming Jew,
    Gall of goat and slips of yew
    Sliver'd in the moon's eclipse,
    Nose of Turk and Tartar's lips,
30   Finger of birth-strangled babe
    Ditch-deliver'd by a drab,
    Make the gruel thick and slab.
    Add thereto a tiger's chaudron,
    For the ingredients of our cauldron.

35 ALL: Double, double, toil and trouble;
    Fire burn and cauldron bubble.

SECOND WITCH: Cool it with a baboon's blood,
    Then the charm is firm and good.

[Enter Hecate to the other three Witches.]

HECATE: O, well done! I commend your pains,
40   And everyone shall share i' the gains.
    And now about the cauldron sing,
    Like elves and fairies in a ring,
    Enchanting all that you put in.
       [Music and a song, "Black spirits." Hecate retires.]

SECOND WITCH: By the pricking of my thumbs,
45   Something wicked this way comes:
    Open, locks,
    Whoever knocks!

ALL: *Double, double, toil and trouble; fire burn and cauldron bubble.*

THIRD WITCH: *A scale from a dragon, a wolf's tooth, a witch's mummy, the stomach and gullet from a ravenous shark from the sea, root of hemlock dug in the dark, the liver from a blaspheming Jew, gallbladder of goat and slips of evergreen slivered in the eclipse of the moon, nose of Turk and a Tartar's lips, a finger of a birth-strangled babe delivered in a ditch by a whore: make our gruel thick and sticky. Add to it a tiger's entrails for the ingredients of our cauldron.*

ALL: *Double, double, toil and trouble; fire burn and cauldron bubble.*

SECOND WITCH: *Cool it with a baboon's blood; now the charm is firm and good.*

[Enter Hecate to the other three Witches.]

HECATE: *O, well done! I commend your efforts, and everyone shall share in the gains. And now sing about the cauldron like elves and fairies in a ring, enchanting all that you have placed there.*
[Music and a song, "Black spirits." Hecate retires.]

SECOND WITCH: *By the pricking of my thumbs, something wicked this way comes. Locks, open for whomever knocks!*

[Enter Macbeth.]

MACBETH: How now, you secret, black, and midnight hags?
    What is't you do?

50   ALL: A deed without a name.

MACBETH: I conjure you, by that which you profess
    Howe'er you come to know it answer me:
    Though you untie the winds and let them fight
    Against the churches, though the yeasty waves
55   Confound and swallow navigation up,
    Though bladed corn be lodged and trees blown down,
    Though castles topple on their warders' heads,
    Though palaces and pyramids do slope
    Their heads to their foundations, though the treasure
60   Of nature's germens tumble all together
    Even till destruction sicken, answer me
    To what I ask you.

FIRST WITCH: Speak.

SECOND WITCH: Demand.

65   THIRD WITCH: We'll answer.

FIRST WITCH: Say, if thou'dst rather hear it from our mouths, or from
    our masters?

MACBETH: Call 'em, let me see 'em.

FIRST WITCH: Pour in sow's blood that hath eaten
70   Her nine farrow; grease that's sweaten
    From the murderer's gibbet throw
    Into the flame.

ALL: Come, high or low;
    Thyself and office deftly show!

[Enter Macbeth.]

MACBETH: *How is it now, you secret, black, and midnight hags? What is it that you do?*

ALL: *A deed without a name.*

MACBETH: *I call you, by that which you say will be true—however you come to know it—answer me. Though you unleash the winds and let them fight against the churches, though the foamy waves confound and swallow navigation up, though blades of corn be knocked down and trees blown over, though castles topple on their master's heads, though palaces and pyramids do slope their heads to their foundations, though the treasure of nature's seeds tumble all together until destruction sickens all, give an answer to what I ask you.*

FIRST WITCH: *Speak.*

SECOND WITCH: *Demand.*

THIRD WITCH: *We'll answer you.*

FIRST WITCH: *Say, if you would rather hear it from our mouths or from our masters?*

MACBETH: *Call them. Let me see them.*

FIRST WITCH: *Pour in the blood of a sow who has eaten her nine piglets; throw into the flame sweat from the murderer taken from him on the gallows.*

ALL: *Come, high or low; show yourself and perform your duty!*

[Thunder. First Apparition, an armed Head.]

75   MACBETH: Tell me, thou unknown power,—

FIRST WITCH: He knows thy thought:
Hear his speech, but say thou nought.

FIRST APPARITION: Macbeth! Macbeth! Macbeth! Beware Macduff;
Beware the Thane of Fife. Dismiss me. Enough.
[Descends.]

80   MACBETH: Whate'er thou art, for thy good caution, thanks;
Thou hast harp'd my fear aright. But one word more–

FIRST WITCH: He will not be commanded. Here's another,
More potent than the first.

[Thunder. Second Apparition, a bloody Child.]

85   SECOND APPARITION: Macbeth! Macbeth! Macbeth!

MACBETH: Had I three ears, I'ld hear thee.

SECOND APPARITION: Be bloody, bold, and resolute; laugh to scorn
The power of man, for none of woman born
Shall harm Macbeth.   *[Descends.]*

90   MACBETH: Then live, Macduff. What need I fear of thee?
But yet I'll make assurance double sure,
And take a bond of fate: thou shalt not live,
That I may tell pale-hearted fear it lies,
And sleep in spite of thunder.

[There is thunder and the first apparition a head in armor, appears.]

MACBETH: *Tell me, you unknown power—*

FIRST WITCH: *He knows what you think. Hear his speech, but don't say anything.*

FIRST APPARITION: *Macbeth! Macbeth! Macbeth! Beware Macduff, beware the lord of Fife. Dismiss me. It is enough.*
[Descends.]

MACBETH: *Whatever you are, thanks for your good caution; you have touched upon my fear. But one word more—*

FIRST WITCH: *He will not be commanded. Here is another, stronger than the first.*

[Thunder and the second apparition, a bloody child, appears.]

SECOND APPARITION: *Macbeth! Macbeth! Macbeth!*

MACBETH: *If I had I three ears, I'd hear you.*

SECOND APPARITION: *Be bloody, bold, and steady. Scorn the power of all men, for no one born of woman shall harm Macbeth.*
[Descends.]

MACBETH: *Then live, Macduff. What reason do I need to fear you? But yet I'll make doubly sure and secure my fate. You shall not live in order that I may tell fear it lies, and I sleep inspite of thunder.*

[Thunder. Third Apparition: a Child crowned, with a tree in his hand.]

95 What is this,
That rises like the issue of a king,
And wears upon his baby brow the round
And top of sovereignty?

ALL: Listen, but speak not to't.

100 **THIRD APPARITION:** Be lion-mettled, proud, and take no care
Who chafes, who frets, or where conspirers are:
Macbeth shall never vanquish'd be until
Great Birnam Wood to high Dunsinane Hill
Shall come against him. *[Descends.]*

105 **MACBETH:** That will never be.
Who can impress the forest, bid the tree
Unfix his earth-bound root? Sweet bodements, good!
Rebellion's head, rise never, till the Wood
Of Birnam rise, and our high-placed Macbeth
110 Shall live the lease of nature, pay his breath
To time and mortal custom. Yet my heart
Throbs to know one thing: tell me, if your art
Can tell so much, shall Banquo's issue ever
Reign in this kingdom?

115 **ALL:** Seek to know no more.

MACBETH: I will be satisfied! Deny me this,
And an eternal curse fall on you! Let me know:
Why sinks that cauldron? and what noise is this?
[Hautboys.]

FIRST WITCH: Show!

120 **SECOND WITCH:** Show!

130

[Thunder. The third apparition appears–a child crowned, with a tree in his hand.]

What is this that rises looking like the son of a king and wearing upon his baby brow the crown?

ALL: *Listen, but do not speak to it.*

THIRD APPARITION: *Be strong as a lion, proud, and don't worry about anything or anyone. You will never be conquered until great Birnam Wood comes to your castle at Dunsinane.*
[Descends.]

MACBETH: *That will never be. Who can make the forest or bid the tree unfix its earth-bound roots? Sweet news is good! Rebellion's head will never rise until the Wood of Birnam moves. Our kingly Macbeth shall live out his natural days, losing his life only to time and mortal custom. Yet my heart throbs to know one more thing. Tell me, if you can tell so much, shall Banquo's children ever reign in this kingdom?*

ALL: *Seek to know no more.*

MACBETH: *I will be satisfied! Deny me this, and an eternal curse fall upon you! Let me know. Why does the cauldron sink and what is this noise?* [Oboes.]

FIRST WITCH: *Show!*

SECOND WITCH: *Show!*

131

THIRD WITCH: Show!

ALL: Show his eyes, and grieve his heart;
　　Come like shadows, so depart!

[A show of eight Kings, the last with a glass in his hand; Banquo's Ghost following.]

125　MACBETH: Thou are too like the spirit of Banquo. Down!
　　　Thy crown does sear mine eyeballs. And thy hair,
　　　Thou other gold-bound brow, is like the first.
　　　A third is like the former. Filthy hags!
　　　Why do you show me this? A fourth! Start, eyes!
130　What, will the line stretch out to the crack of doom?
　　　Another yet! A seventh! I'll see no more:
　　　And yet the eighth appears, who bears a glass
　　　Which shows me many more; and some I see
　　　That twofold balls and treble sceptres carry:
135　Horrible sight! Now I see 'tis true;
　　　For the blood-bolter'd Banquo smiles upon me,
　　　And points at them for his. What, is this so?

　　FIRST WITCH: Ay, sir, all this is so. But why
140　Stands Macbeth thus amazedly?
　　　Come, sisters, cheer we up his sprites,
　　　And show the best of our delights.
　　　I'll charm the air to give a sound,
　　　While you perform your antic round,
145　That this great King may kindly say
　　　Our duties did his welcome pay.

[Music. The Witches dance and then vanish with Hecate.]

MACBETH: Where are they? Gone? Let this pernicious hour
　　Stand aye accursed in the calendar!
　　Come in, without there!

132

THIRD WITCH: Show!

ALL: Show his eyes and grieve his heart; come let us depart like shadows.

[There appears a line of eight kings, the last with a mirror in his hand; Banquo's ghost follows.]

MACBETH: You look too much like Banquo. Down! Your crown sears my eyeballs. And your hair—you also have golden hair, just like the first one. A third is just like him too. Filthy hags! Why do you show me this? A fourth! Stop it, eyes! What, will this line of kings stretch out to the end of time? Yet another! A seventh! I'll see no more! And yet the eighth appears who bears a mirror which shows me many more. Some I see carry double balls and triple scepters–the signs of Scotland and Wales–too. Horrible sight! Now I see it is true; for the blood-spattered Banquo smiles at me and points at those images as his. What, is all this to come to pass?

FIRST WITCH: Ay, sir, all this is so. But why stand there amazed? Come, sisters, cheer up his spirits and show him the best of our charms. I'll manipulate the air to give a sound while you perform your dance so that this great King may say most kindly that we did our duties.

[Music. The witches dance and then vanish with Hecate.]

MACBETH: Where are they? Gone? Let this evil hour stand cursed in the calendar! Come in, whoever is there!

[Enter Lennox.]

150 LENNOX: What's your Grace's will?

MACBETH: Saw you the weird sisters?

LENNOX: No, my lord.

MACBETH: Came they not by you?

LENNOX: No indeed, my lord.

155 MACBETH: Infected be the air whereon they ride,
And damn'd all those that trust them! I did hear
The galloping of horse. Who was't came by?

LENNOX: 'Tis two or three, my lord, that bring you word
Macduff is fled to England.

160 MACBETH: Fled to England?

LENNOX: Ay, my good lord.

MACBETH: *[Aside.]* Time, thou anticipatest my dread exploits.
The flighty purpose never is o'ertook
Unless the deed go with it. From this moment
165 The very firstlings of my heart shall be
The firstlings of my hand. And even now,
To crown my thoughts with acts, be it thought and done:
The castle of Macduff I will surprise,
Seize upon Fife; give to the edge o' the sword
170 His wife, his babes, and all unfortunate souls
That trace him in his line. No boasting like a fool;
This deed I'll do before this purpose cool.
But no more sights!–Where are these gentlemen?
Come, bring me where they are.

[Exeunt.]

[Enter Lennox.]

LENNOX: *What's your Grace's pleasure?*

MACBETH: *Did you see the witches?*

LENNOX: *No, my lord.*

MACBETH: *Did they not come by you?*

LENNOX: *No indeed, my lord.*

MACBETH: *The very air they ride is plagued, and damned be all who trust them! I did hear the galloping of horses. Who was it who came by?*

LENNOX: *It was two or three, my lord, who brought you word that Macduff has fled to England.*

MACBETH: *Fled to England?*

LENNOX: *Ay, my good lord.*

MACBETH: [Aside.] *Time, you anticipate my dreadful deeds. Purpose is never fulfilled unless the deed is finished too. From this moment on the very first things I feel in my heart shall be the first things my hands do. And even now, I shall follow my thoughts with acts so that they will be complete; I will surprise the castle of Macduff, seize upon Fife, kill everyone—his wife, his babies, and all those unfortunate souls who trace him in his line. I will not boast like a fool. This deed I'll do before my purpose cools. No more sights! Where are these gentlemen? Come, bring me to them.*

[Exit.]

SCENE 2

Fife. Macduff's castle.

[Enter Lady Macduff, her Son, and Ross.]

LADY MACDUFF: What had he done, to make him fly the land?

ROSS: You must have patience, madam.

LADY MACDUFF: He had none;
    His flight was madness. When our actions do not,
5   Our fears do make us traitors.

ROSS: You know not
    Whether it was his wisdom or his fear.

LADY MACDUFF: Wisdom? To leave his wife, to leave his babes,
    His mansion, and his titles, in a place
10   From whence himself does fly? He loves us not;
    He wants the natural touch: for the poor wren,
    The most diminutive of birds, will fight,
    Her young ones in her nest, against the owl.
    All is the fear and nothing is the love;
15   As little is the wisdom, where the flight
    So runs against all reason.

ROSS: My dearest coz,
    I pray you, school yourself. But for your husband,
    He is noble, wise, judicious, and best knows
20   The fits o' the season. I dare not speak much further;
    But cruel are the times, when we are traitors
    And do not know ourselves; when we hold rumor
    From what we fear, yet know not what we fear,
    But float upon a wild and violent sea
25   Each way and move. I take my leave of you;
    Shall not be long but I'll be here again.
    Things at the worst will cease, or else climb upward
    To what they were before. My pretty cousin,
    Blessing upon you!

SCENE 2

Fife. Macduff's castle.

[Enter Lady Macduff, her son, and Ross.]

LADY MACDUFF: *What had he done to make him flee the country?*

ROSS: *You must have patience, madam.*

LADY MACDUFF: *He had none; his flight was madness. When our actions do not make us traitors, our fears do.*

ROSS: *You do not know whether it was his wisdom or his fear.*

LADY MACDUFF: *Wisdom? To leave his wife, to leave his babies, his castle, and his titles in a place from which he himself flies? He does not love us. He lacks natural affection. Even the poor wren, the smallest of birds, will fight against the owl when she has her young ones in her nest. He has much fear and no love for us, since there is little wisdom where flight runs against all reason.*

ROSS: *My dearest cousin, I pray you, control yourself. Your husband is noble, wise, judicious, and best knows the fits of the season. I dare not speak much further. But cruel are these times when we are traitors and do not know ourselves; when we believe rumor only because we fear. Yet we don't know what we fear, but instead float upon a wild and violent sea tossing each and every way. I take my leave of you. It shall not be long until I'll be here again. These terrible things will cease or else reverse themselves to what they were before. My pretty cousin, blessing upon you!*

30 LADY MACDUFF: Father'd he is, and yet he's fatherless.

ROSS: I am so much a fool, should I stay longer,
It would be my disgrace and your discomfort.
I take my leave at once.

[Exit.]

LADY MACDUFF: Sirrah, your father's dead.
35 And what will you do now? How will you live?

SON: As birds do, Mother.

LADY MACDUFF: What, with worms and flies?

SON: With what I get, I mean; and so do they.

LADY MACDUFF: Poor bird! Thou'ldst never fear the net nor lime,
40 The pitfall nor the gin.

SON: Why should I, Mother? Poor birds they are not set for.
My father is not dead, for all your saying.

LADY MACDUFF: Yes, he is dead. How wilt thou do for a father?

SON: Nay, how will you do for a husband?

45 LADY MACDUFF: Why, I can buy me twenty at any market.

SON: Then you'll buy 'em to sell again.

LADY MACDUFF: Thou speak'st with all thy wit, and yet, i' faith,
With wit enough for thee.

SON: Was my father a traitor, Mother?

50 LADY MACDUFF: Ay, that he was.

138

LADY MACDUFF: [Looking at her son.] *He has a father, and yet he's fatherless.*

ROSS: *I am so much a fool. If I should stay longer, it would be my disgrace and your discomfort. I will take my leave at once.*

[Exit.]

LADY MACDUFF: *Young man, your father's dead. What will you do now? How will you live?*

SON: *As birds do, mother.*

LADY MACDUFF: *What, by eating worms and flies?*

SON: *With what I get, I mean, and so do they.*

LADY MACDUFF: *You poor bird! You will never fear the net, lime, pit or snare used to capture birds.*

SON: *Why should I, mother? Poor birds are not trapped. My father is not dead, despite your saying it.*

LADY MACDUFF: *Yes, he is dead. How will you do for a father?*

SON: *No, mother, how will you do for a husband?*

LADY MACDUFF: *Why, I can buy twenty for myself at any market.*

SON: *Then you'll buy them to sell again, for you will not be happy.*

LADY MACDUFF: *I can't believe how you talk!*

SON: *Was my father a traitor, mother?*

LADY MACDUFF: *Yes, that he was.*

SON: What is a traitor?

LADY MACDUFF: Why, one that swears and lies.

SON: And be all traitors that do so?

LADY MACDUFF: Everyone that does so is a traitor and must be
hanged.

55   SON: And must they all be hanged that swear and lie?

LADY MACDUFF: Every one.

SON: Who must hang them?

LADY MACDUFF: Why, the honest men.

SON: Then the liars and swearers are fools; for there are liars and
60   swearers enough to beat the honest men and hang up them.

LADY MACDUFF: Now, God help thee, poor monkey! But how wilt
thou do for a father?

SON: If he were dead, you'ld weep for him: if you would not, it were
a good sign that I should quickly have a new father.

65   LADY MACDUFF: Poor prattler, how thou talk'st!

[Enter a Messenger.]

MESSENGER: Bless you, fair dame! I am not to you known,
Though, in your state of honor I am perfect.
I doubt some danger does approach you nearly.
If you will take a homely man's advice,
70   Be not found here; hence, with your little ones.
To fright you thus, methinks I am too savage;
To do worse to you were fell cruelty,

140

SON: *What is a traitor?*

LADY MACDUFF: *Why, one that swears and lies.*

SON: *And are all that do so traitors?*

LADY MACDUFF: *Everyone that does so is a traitor and must be hanged.*

SON: *And must they all be hanged that swear and lie?*

LADY MACDUFF: *Every one.*

SON: *Who must hang them?*

LADY MACDUFF: *Why, the honest men.*

SON: *Then the liars and swearers are fools, for there are enough liars and swearers to beat the honest men and hang them up instead.*

LADY MACDUFF: *God help you, poor monkey! But how will you do for a father?*

SON: *If he were dead, you would weep for him; if you would not, it would be a good sign that I should quickly have a new father.*

LADY MACDUFF: *Poor prattler, how you talk!*

[Enter a Messenger.]

MESSENGER: *Bless you, fair lady. Although I am not known to you, I am fully aware of your present state. I believe some danger approaches you very quickly. If you will take an ordinary man's advice, leave immediately with your children! I'm sorry I have*

Which is too nigh your person. Heaven preserve you!
I dare abide no longer.

[Exit.]

75   **Lady Macduff:** Whither should I fly?
I have done no harm. But I remember now
I am in this earthly world, where to do harm
Is often laudable, to do good sometime
Accounted dangerous folly. Why then, alas,
80   Do I put up that womanly defense,
To say I have done no harm?—What are these faces?

[Enter Murderers.]

First Murderer: Where is your husband?

Lady Macduff: I hope, in no place so unsanctified
Where such as thou mayst find him.

85   **First Murderer:** He's a traitor.

Son: Thou liest, thou shag-ear'd villain!

First Murderer: What, you egg!
                    [Stabs him.]
  Young fry of treachery!

Son: He has kill'd me, Mother.
90   Run away, I pray you!   *[Dies.]*

[Exit Lady Macduff, crying "Murder!"]

[Exeunt murderers, following her.]

frightened you with my warning, but to do otherwise would be cruel. Heaven preserve you! I dare stay no longer.

[Exit.]

LADY MACDUFF: *Where should I fly? I have done nothing wrong. But I remember now that I am in this earthly world where to do harm is often praiseworthy and to do good sometimes amounts to dangerous folly. Why do I put up that womanly defense to say I have done no harm—who are you men?*

[Enter Murderers.]

FIRST MURDERER: *Where is your husband?*

LADY MACDUFF: *I hope in no place so unholy as this where such as you might find him.*

FIRST MURDERER: *He's a traitor.*

SON: *You lie, you shaggy villain!*

FIRST MURDERER: *What, you egg!*
                              [Stabs him.]
  Young fry of treachery!

SON: *He has mortally wounded me. Mother, run away. Please!*
                              [Dies.]

[Exit Lady Macduff, crying "Murder!"]

[Exit murderers following her.]

SCENE 3
England. Before the King's palace.

[Enter Malcolm and Macduff.]

MALCOLM: Let us seek out some desolate shade and there
    Weep our sad bosoms empty.

MACDUFF: Let us rather
    Hold fast the mortal sword, and like good men
5   Bestride our downfall'n birthdom. Each new morn
    New widows howl, new orphans cry, new sorrows
    Strike heaven on the face, that it resounds
    As if it felt with Scotland and yell'd out
    Like syllable of dolor.

10   MALCOLM: What I believe, I'll wail;
    What know, believe; and what I can redress,
    As I shall find the time to friend, I will.
    What you have spoke, it may be so perchance.
    This tyrant, whose sole name blisters our tongues,
15   Was once thought honest. You have loved him well;
    He hath not touch'd you yet. I am young, but some thing
    You may deserve of him through me, and wisdom
    To offer up a weak, poor, innocent lamb
    To appease an angry god.

20   MACDUFF: I am not treacherous.

MALCOLM: But Macbeth is.
    A good and virtuous nature may recoil
    In an imperial charge. But I shall crave your pardon;
    That which you are, my thoughts cannot transpose.
25   Angels are bright still, though the brightest fell.
    Though all things foul would wear the brows of grace,
    Yet grace must still look so.

SCENE 3

England. Before the King's palace.

[Enter Malcolm and Macduff.]

MALCOLM: *Let us seek out some desolate shade and there cry ourselves empty.*

MACDUFF: *Let us rather hold fast our deadly swords and, like the good men we are, stride through our down-trodden Scotland. Each new morning brings new news of widows, orphans, sorrows. Heaven has reacted as if it, too, felt the pain of Scotland.*

MALCOLM: *What I believe, I'll lament. I'll set it right when the time is right. What you have spoken may indeed be true. This tyrant whose very name blisters our tongues was once thought to be honest. You have loved him well, Macduff. He has not harmed you yet. I am young, but you may gain favor from him by offering me up as a sacrifice to him.*

MACDUFF: *I am not treacherous.*

MALCOLM: *But Macbeth is. A good and virtuous nature may - buckle under an imperial command. But I shall beg your pardon. My thought cannot change your true nature. Angels are still bright even though the brightest have fallen. Macbeth may wear the crown and look like a king, yet I must still act my part.*

MACDUFF: I have lost my hopes.

MALCOLM: Perchance even there where I did find my doubts.
30   Why in that rawness left you wife and child,
    Those precious motives, those strong knots of love,
    Without leave-taking? I pray you,
    Let not my jealousies be your dishonors,
    But mine own safeties. You may be rightly just,
35   Whatever I shall think.

MACDUFF: Bleed, bleed, poor country!
    Great tyranny, lay thou thy basis sure,
    For goodness dare not check thee. Wear thou thy wrongs;
    The title is affeer'd. Fare thee well, lord.
40   I would not be the villain that thou think'st
    For the whole space that's in the tyrant's grasp
    And the rich East to boot.

MALCOLM: Be not offended;
    I speak not as in absolute fear of you.
45   I think our country sinks beneath the yoke;
    It weeps, it bleeds, and each new day a gash
    Is added to her wounds. I think withal
    There would be hands uplifted in my right;
    And here from gracious England have I offer
50   Of goodly thousands. But for all this,
    When I shall tread upon the tyrant's head,
    Or wear it on my sword, yet my poor country
    Shall have more vices than it had before,
    More suffer and more sundry ways than ever,
55   By him that shall succeed.

MACDUFF: What should he be?

MALCOLM: It is myself I mean, in whom I know
    All the particulars of vice so grafted
    That, when they shall be open'd, black Macbeth
60   Will seem as pure as snow, and the poor state

MACDUFF: *I have lost my hopes.*

MALCOLM: *Perhaps you did even as I did find my doubts. Why have you left your wife and children—all that is precious to you—without a word in parting? I beg you, understand that my own safety rules my thinking. You may be righteous, despite what I think.*

MACDUFF: *Bleed, bleed, poor country! The great tyranny lays your base firmly since goodness dares not check him. He wears his stolen powers; your title is confirmed.* [Makes ready to leave.] *Farewell, lord. I would not be the villain that you think I am for everything in the tyrant's grasp and the rich East yet to come.*

MALCOLM: *Do not be offended; I do not speak in absolute fear of you. I think our country sinks beneath the yoke of oppression. It weeps, it bleeds, and a new injury is added to her wounds every day. I think, though, that there will be hands raised in my just cause. I have been offered thousands from England. But despite all this, when I shall tread upon the tyrant's head or wear that head upon my sword, my poor country will have more problems than it ever had before. More will suffer and in more ways than ever, under the rule of the king that shall succeed Macbeth.*

MACDUFF: *Who do you mean?*

MALCOLM: *It is myself I mean. I know so many evil vices are entwined in me that when they are released, black Macbeth will seem as pure as snow. Our poor country will think him to be like a lamb compared to my evils.*

Esteem him as a lamb, being compared
With my confineless harms.

MACDUFF: Not in the legions
Of horrid hell can come a devil more damn'd
65   In evils to top Macbeth.

MALCOLM: I grant him bloody,
Luxurious, avaricious, false, deceitful,
Sudden, malicious, smacking of every sin
That has a name. But there's no bottom, none,
70   In my voluptuousness. Your wives, your daughters,
Your matrons, and your maids could not fill up
The cistern of my lust, and my desire
All continent impediments would o'erbear
That did oppose my will. Better Macbeth
75   Than such an one to reign.

MACDUFF: Boundless intemperance
In nature is a tyranny; it hath been
The untimely emptying of the happy throne,
And fall of many kings. But fear not yet
80   To take upon you what is yours. You may
Convey your pleasures in a spacious plenty
And yet seem cold, the time you may so hoodwink.
We have willing dames enough; there cannot be
That vulture in you, to devour so many
85   As will to greatness dedicate themselves,
Finding it so inclined.

MALCOLM: With this there grows
In my most ill-composed affection such
A stanchless avarice that, were I King,
90   I should cut off the nobles for their lands,
Desire his jewels and this other's house,
And my more-having would be as a sauce
To make me hunger more, that I should forge
Quarrels unjust against the good and loyal,
95   Destroying them for wealth.

MACDUFF: *There is no devil in hell who can be more damned than Macbeth.*

MALCOLM: *I grant him to be bloody, lusty, greedy, false and deceitful, sudden, malicious, smacking of every sin that has a name. But there's no bottom, none, to my sexuality. Your wives, daughters, mothers, and your maids could not quench my lust. My sexual appetites will not be controlled by any including myself. Better let Macbeth reign than one like me.*

MACDUFF: *Lack of self-control is indeed an absolute hell. It has caused the untimely fall of kings and kingdoms. But do not fear to take what is yours. You may convey your pleasures in the spacious plenty of our land and still appear pure. You can indeed fool our time. We have willing women enough. You cannot imagine how may women would be glad to share your lust.*

MALCOLM: *But there also grows in me a great greed so that, were I King, I should cut off the nobles from their lands, take one's valuables and another's house. The more I would have, the more I would desire. I would destroy our lords for the wealth I could gain.*

MACDUFF: This avarice
 Sticks deeper, grows with more pernicious root
 Than summer-seeming lust, and it hath been
 The sword of our slain kings. Yet do not fear;
100 Scotland hath foisons to fill up your will
 Of your mere own. All these are portable,
 With other graces weigh'd.

MALCOLM: But I have none. The king-becoming graces,
 As justice, verity, temperance, stableness,
105 Bounty, perseverance, mercy, lowliness,
 Devotion, patience, courage, fortitude,
 I have no relish of them, but abound
 In the division of each several crime,
 Acting it many ways. Nay, had I power, I should
110 Pour the sweet milk of concord into hell,
 Uproar the universal peace, confound
 All unity on earth.

MACDUFF: O Scotland, Scotland!

MALCOLM: If such a one be fit to govern, speak.
115 I am as I have spoken.

MACDUFF: Fit to govern?
 No, not to live. O nation miserable!
 With an untitled tyrant bloody-scepter'd,
 When shalt thou see thy wholesome days again,
120 Since that the truest issue of thy throne
 By his own interdiction stands accursed,
 And does blaspheme his breed? Thy royal father
 Was a most sainted king: the queen that bore thee,
 Oftener upon her knees than on her feet,
125 Died every day she lived. Fare thee well!
 These evils thou repeat'st upon thyself
 Have banish'd me from Scotland. O my breast,
 Thy hope ends here!

MACDUFF: This greed sticks deeper and grows with a stronger root than mere sexuality, and it has been the past way of our slain kings. Yet do not fear; Scotland has riches to fill up your will beyond belief. All these can be carried if you weigh them against your better attributes.

MALCOLM: But I have none. Kingly graces such as justice, truth, temperance, stableness, generosity, perseverance, mercy, humbleness, devotion, patience, courage, and fortitude are not mixed in me. Rather, I abound in crimes which take many forms. If I had the power, I would destroy all agreements and peace and turn our country into anarchy.

MACDUFF: O Scotland, Scotland!

MALCOLM: If such a one is fit to govern, speak to me. I am just as I have spoken.

MACDUFF: Fit to govern? No, you are not fit to live. O, nation in misery! We have a tyrant on the throne, and we may never see wholesome days again. By your own words, you are unfit to govern properly. Your royal father was a sainted king; the queen who bore you was more often on her knees in prayer than living in a royal world. Farewell! The evils you repeatedly brag about have banished me from Scotland. O, my heart—your hope ends here!

MALCOLM: Macduff, this noble passion,
130   Child of integrity, hath from my soul
Wiped the black scruples, reconciled my thoughts
To thy good truth and honor. Devilish Macbeth
By many of these trains hath sought to win me
Into his power, and modest wisdom plucks me
135   From over-credulous haste. But God above
Deal between thee and me! For even now
I put myself to thy direction and
Unspeak mine own detraction; here abjure
The taints and blames I laid upon myself,
140   For strangers to my nature. I am yet
Unknown to woman, never was forsworn,
Scarcely have coveted what was mine own,
At no time broke my faith, would not betray
The devil to his fellow, and delight
145   No less in truth than life. My first false speaking
Was this upon myself. What I am truly,
Is thine and my poor country's to command:
Whither indeed, before thy here-approach,
Old Siward, with ten thousand warlike men,
150   Already at a point, was setting forth.
Now we'll together, and the chance of goodness
Be like our warranted quarrel! Why are you silent?

MACDUFF: Such welcome and unwelcome things at once
'Tis hard to reconcile.

[Enter a Doctor.]

155 MALCOLM: Well, more anon. Comes the King forth, I pray you?

DOCTOR: Ay, sir, there are a crew of wretched souls
That stay his cure. Their malady convinces
The great assay of art, but at his touch,
Such sanctity hath heaven given his hand,
160   They presently amend.

MALCOLM: Macduff, your noble passion, which is obviously genuine, has wiped away my doubts and convinced me of your honorable intention. Devilish Macbeth has tried to trick me into returning to Scotland, and I must be overly cautious. But God above can deal between you and me! I now put myself in your direction and also take back all I've said previously. Forget all the terrible things I've said about myself. I am a virgin and I do not covet the property of others; I am deeply religious and would not betray anyone. I delight in truth as much as I delight in life. In fact, the first lie I spoke was just now when I falsely accused myself of terrible crimes. What I am is yours to command. Indeed, old Siward is just now setting out with ten thousand soldiers for Scotland. We can go together, and our chances are as good as our just quarrel! Why are you silent?

MACDUFF: Such welcome and unwelcome things coming all at once are hard to reconcile.

[Enter a Doctor.]

MALCOLM: Well, we will speak more in just a bit. [To doctor.] Does the King come now, tell me, if you please?

DOCTOR: Yes, sir. There are wretched souls who wait for his cure. Their illness convinces them that this English King's touch will cure them of their sickness. Heaven has blessed him with the touch of healing powers.

MALCOLM: I thank you, Doctor.   *[Exit Doctor.]*

MACDUFF: What's the disease he means?

MALCOLM: 'Tis call'd the evil:
    A most miraculous work in this good King,
165   Which often, since my here-remain in England,
    I have seen him do. How he solicits heaven,
    Himself best knows; but strangely-visited people,
    All swol'n and ulcerous, pitiful to the eye,
    The mere despair of surgery, he cures,
170   Hanging a golden stamp about their necks,
    Put on with holy prayers: and 'tis spoken,
    To the succeeding royalty he leaves
    The healing benediction. With this strange virtue
    He hath a heavenly gift of prophecy,
175   And sundry blessings hang about his throne
    That speak him full of grace.

[Enter Ross.]

MACDUFF: See, who comes here?

MALCOLM: My countryman: but yet I know him not.

MACDUFF: My ever gentle cousin, welcome hither.

180   MALCOLM: I know him now. Good God, betimes remove
    The means that makes us strangers!

ROSS: Sir, amen.

MACDUFF: Stands Scotland where it did?

ROSS: Alas, poor country,
185   Almost afraid to know itself! It cannot
    Be call'd our mother, but our grave. Where nothing,
    But who knows nothing, is once seen to smile;

MALCOLM: *I thank you, Doctor.*   [Exit Doctor.]

MACDUFF: *What's the disease he means?*

MALCOLM: *It is called scrofula. A most miraculous work is there in this king who I have often seen heal people with this disease. How he does this in heaven's name I cannot say. However, these swollen and ulcerous people who are beyond hope are cured when he hangs prayers around their necks. He has the gift of prophesy also, and the heavens smile on his rule.*

[Enter Ross.]

MACDUFF: *Look. Who comes here?*

MALCOLM: *My countryman, but yet I do not know him.*

MACDUFF: *My ever gentle cousin, welcome.*

MALCOLM: *I know him now. Good God. I hope we can remove the evil that makes us strangers!*

ROSS: *Sir, amen.*

MACDUFF: *Does Scotland stand where it did?*

ROSS: *Alas, poor country. It is almost afraid to know itself! It cannot be called our mother, but rather our grave. No one is enjoying life at present. No smiles; but rather groans, moans, and shrieks split the air. Mere sorrow seems almost a wonderful expe-*

Where sighs and groans and shrieks that rend the air,
Are made, not mark'd; where violent sorrow seems
190　　　A modern ecstasy. The dead man's knell
Is there scarce ask'd for who, and good men's lives
Expire before the flowers in their caps,
Dying or ere they sicken.

MACDUFF: O, relation
195　　　Too nice, and yet too true!

MALCOLM: What's the newest grief?

ROSS: That of an hour's age doth hiss the speaker;
Each minute teems a new one.

MACDUFF: How does my wife?

200　　ROSS: Why, well.

MACDUFF: And all my children?

ROSS: Well too.

MACDUFF: The tyrant has not batter'd at their peace?

ROSS: No; they were well at peace when I did leave 'em.

205　　MACDUFF: Be not a niggard of your speech. How goes't?

ROSS: When I came hither to transport the tidings,
Which I have heavily borne, there ran a rumor
Of many worthy fellows that were out,
Which was to my belief witness'd the rather,
210　　　For that I saw the tyrant's power a-foot:
Now is the time of help; your eye in Scotland
Would create soldiers, make our women fight,
To doff their dire distresses.

rience. We have no time to mourn all of our dead, and the lives of good men are cut short before their time.

MACDUFF: Indeed, it is just too true.

MALCOLM: What's the newest grief?

ROSS: It seems like every hour brings a new problem and each minute begins a new one.

MACDUFF: How does my wife?

ROSS: Why, well.

MACDUFF: And all my children?

ROSS: Well, too.

MACDUFF: The tyrant has not battered at their peace?

ROSS: No, they were certainly at peace when I did leave them.

MACDUFF: Do not be so stingy with your speech. How is it going?

ROSS: [To Malcolm.] When I came here to carry some heavy news, a rumor was circulating about many men who were in open rebellion against Macbeth. I believe it is so since I saw Macbeth's power in the land. Now is the right time to strike. Your presence in Scotland would create soldiers, make even our women fight to rid themselves of our current problems.

MALCOLM: Be't their comfort
215   We are coming thither. Gracious England hath
Lent us good Siward and ten thousand men;
An older and a better soldier none
That Christendom gives out.

ROSS: Would I could answer
220   This comfort with the like! But I have words
That would be howl'd out in the desert air,
Where hearing should not latch them.

MACDUFF: What concern they?
The general cause? Or is it a fee-grief
225   Due to some single breast?

ROSS: No mind that's honest
But in it shares some woe, though the main part
Pertains to you alone.

MACDUFF: If it be mine,
230   Keep it not from me, quickly let me have it.

ROSS: Let not your ears despise my tongue for ever,
Which shall possess them with the heaviest sound
That ever yet they heard.

MACDUFF: Humh! I guess at it.

235 ROSS: Your castle is surprised; your wife and babes
Savagely slaughter'd. To relate the manner
Were, on the quarry of these murder'd deer,
To add the death of you.

MALCOLM: Merciful heaven!
240   What, man! Ne'er pull your hat upon your brows;
Give sorrow words. The grief that does not speak
Whispers the o'er fraught heart, and bids it break.

MALCOLM: *We are coming there to comfort them. Gracious England has lent us good Siward and ten thousand soldiers. There is not an older or better soldier in all the land.*

ROSS: *I wish I could answer this comfort with similar news! But I have words that should be howled out in the desert air where hearing could not catch them.*

MACDUFF: *Whom do they concern? Is it a general problem, or is it only a grief for a single individual?*

ROSS: *Everyone shares some of the woe, but the main part pertains to you alone.*

MACDUFF: *If it is mine, don't keep it from me, but quickly let me have it.*

ROSS: *Let your ears not despise my tongue forever. I will give them the heaviest sound that they have ever heard.*

MACDUFF: *Humh! I guess at it.*

ROSS: *Your castle is taken; your wife and babies are savagely slaughtered. To relate the manner of their deaths would add more misery to you in this troubling time.*

MALCOLM: *Merciful heaven! What, man! Do not pull your hat upon your brows. Give your sorrow words. The grief that does not speak whispers to the heart and will break it in two.*

MACDUFF: My children too?

ROSS: Wife, children, servants, all
245   That could be found.

MACDUFF: And I must be from thence!
    My wife kill'd too?

ROSS: I have said.

MALCOLM: Be comforted.
250   Let's make us medicines of our great revenge,
    To cure this deadly grief.

MACDUFF: He has no children. All my pretty ones?
    Did you say all? O hell-kite! All?
    What, all my pretty chickens and their dam
255   At one fell swoop?

MALCOLM: Dispute it like a man.

MACDUFF: I shall do so;
    But I must also feel it as a man.
    I cannot but remember such things were,
260   That were most precious to me. Did heaven look on,
    And would not take their part? Sinful Macduff,
    They were all struck for thee! Naught that I am,
    Not for their own demerits, but for mine,
    Fell slaughter on their souls. Heaven rest them now!

265 MALCOLM: Be this the whetstone of your sword. Let grief
    Convert to anger; blunt not the heart, enrage it.

MACDUFF: O, I could play the woman with mine eyes,
    And braggart with my tongue! But, gentle heavens,
    Cut short all intermission; front to front
270   Bring thou this fiend of Scotland and myself;
    Within my sword's length set him; if he 'scape,
    Heaven forgive him too!

160

MACDUFF: *My children, too?*

ROSS: *Wife, children, servants, all that could be found.*

MACDUFF: *And I have left that place! My wife killed, too?*

ROSS: *I have said it.*

MALCOLM: *Be comforted. Let's make medicine of our great revenge and cure this deadly grief.*

MACDUFF: *Macbeth has no children I can go after. All my pretty ones? Did you say all? O, fiend of hell! All? What, all my pretty chickens and their mother at one fell swoop?*

MALCOLM: *Dispute it like a man.*

MACDUFF: *I shall do so, but I must also feel it as a man. I cannot but remember such things which were more precious to me. Why did heaven see this and not defend them? Sinful Macduff, they were all killed for you! Not that I was struck down. Not for their own wrongdoing, but for mine instead, did this slaughter fall on their souls. May they rest in heaven.*

MALCOLM: *Let this sharpen your sword. Let grief convert to anger. Do not blunt the heart now; enrage it.*

MACDUFF: *O, I could play the woman with my eyes and cry or talk tough with my tongue! But, gentle heavens, cut short all that stands in my way. Bring this fiend of Scotland and myself into combat with each other. Set him in front of me. If he escapes, heaven should forgive him also.*

MALCOLM: This tune goes manly.
 Come, go we to the King; our power is ready;
275 Our lack is nothing but our leave. Macbeth
 Is ripe for shaking, and the powers above
 Put on their instruments. Receive what cheer you may;
 The night is long that never finds the day.

[Exeunt.]

❦

MALCOLM: *This tune goes manly. Come, we go to see the King. Our power is ready. We lack nothing except our departure. Macbeth is ripe for shaking, and the powers in heaven now make ready their instruments. Receive what cheer you may in these facts, since no matter the length of the night, day will always follow.*

[Exit.]

ACT V

SCENE 1
Dunsinane. Anteroom in the castle.

[Enter a Doctor of Physic and a Waiting Gentlewoman.]

DOCTOR: I have two nights watched with you, but can perceive no truth in your report. When was it she last walked?

GENTLEWOMAN: Since his Majesty went into the field, I have seen her rise from her bed, throw her nightgown upon her, unlock her
5   closet, take forth paper, fold it, write upon't, read it, afterwards seal it, and again return to bed; yet all this while in a most fast sleep.

DOCTOR: A great perturbation in nature, to receive at once the benefit of sleep and do the effects of watching! In this slumbery agitation, besides her walking and other actual performances, what, at
10   any time, have you heard her say?

GENTLEWOMAN: That, sir, which I will not report after her.

DOCTOR: You may to me, and 'tis most meet you should.

GENTLEWOMAN: Neither to you nor any one, having no witness to confirm my speech.

[Enter Lady Macbeth, with a taper.]

15   Lo you, here she comes! This is her very guise, and, upon my life, fast asleep. Observe her; stand close.

ACT V

SCENE 1

Dunsinane. Anteroom in the castle.

[Enter a Doctor and a Waiting Gentlewoman.]

DOCTOR: *I have watched with you for two nights, but can understand no truth from your report. When did she last walk?*

GENTLEWOMAN: *Since his Majesty went into the field, I have seen her rise from her bed, throw on her nightgown, unlock her closet, take out paper, fold it, write upon it, read it, seal it, and again return to bed. Yet, she does all this while in a deep sleep.*

DOCTOR: *A strange disturbance this is, to have the benefit of sleep and yet perform tasks. In this disturbed sleep, besides her walking and other actual things, what, at any time, have you heard her say as she sleepwalks?*

GENTLEWOMAN: *That, sir, which I will not report about her.*

DOCTOR: *You may to me, and it is most proper that you should.*

GENTLEWOMAN: *Neither to you nor anyone else since I have no witness to confirm my words.*

[Enter Lady Macbeth with a taper.]

Look! Here she comes! This is her very look; and, upon my life, she is fast asleep. Observe her; stand close.

DOCTOR: How came she by that light?

GENTLEWOMAN: Why, it stood by her. She has light by her continually; 'tis her command.

20 DOCTOR: You see, her eyes are open.

GENTLEWOMAN: Ay, but their sense is shut.

DOCTOR: What is it she does now? Look how she rubs her hands.

GENTLEWOMAN: It is an accustomed action with her, to seem thus washing her hands. I have known her continue in this a quarter of
25 an hour.

LADY MACBETH: Yet here's a spot.

DOCTOR: Hark, she speaks! I will set down what comes from her, to satisfy my remembrance the more strongly.

LADY MACBETH: Out, damned spot! Out, I say! One–two--why then
30 'tis time to do't. Hell is murky. Fie, my lord, fie! A soldier, and afeard? What need we fear who knows it, when none can call our power to account? Yet who would have thought the old man to have had so much blood in him?

DOCTOR: Do you mark that?

35 LADY MACBETH: The Thane of Fife had a wife; where is she now? What, will these hands ne'er be clean? No more o' that, my lord, no more o' that. You mar all with this starting.

DOCTOR: Go to, go to; you have known what you should not.

GENTLEWOMAN: She has spoke what she should not, I am sure of that.
40 Heaven knows what she has known.

DOCTOR: *How did she come by that light?*

GENTLEWOMAN: *Why, it stood by her. She has light by her at all times. It is her order.*

DOCTOR: *You see, her eyes are open.*

GENTLEWOMAN: *Yes, but they do not see.*

DOCTOR: *What is it she does now? Look how she rubs her hands.*

GENTLEWOMAN: *It is an accustomed action with her, to pantomine washing her hands. I have known her to continue in this for a quarter of an hour.*

LADY MACBETH: *Yet here's a spot.*

DOCTOR: *Hark, she speaks! I will write down what she says to satisfy my memory.*

LADY MACBETH: *Out, damned spot! Out, I say! One—two—why then it is time to do it. Hell is murky. Shame, my lord, shame! A soldier, and afraid? Why do we fear who knows what we have done, when no one can equal our power? Yet who would have thought the old man would have had so much blood in him?*

DOCTOR: *Do you note that?*

LADY MACBETH: *The lord of Fife had a wife; where is she now? What, will these hands never be clean again? No more of that, my lord, no more of that. You destroy the mood with this strange fit.*

DOCTOR: *Enough. Enough. You know what you should not.*

GENTLEWOMAN: *She has spoken what she should not, I am sure of that. Heaven knows what she has known.*

167

LADY MACBETH: Here's the smell of the blood still. All the perfumes of Arabia will not sweeten this little hand. Oh, oh, oh!

DOCTOR: What a sigh is there! The heart is sorely charged.

45 GENTLEWOMAN: I would not have such a heart in my bosom for the dignity of the whole body.

DOCTOR: Well, well, well—

GENTLEWOMAN: Pray God it be, sir.

DOCTOR: This disease is beyond my practice. Yet I have known those which have walked in their sleep who have died holily in their
50 beds.

LADY MACBETH: Wash your hands, put on your nightgown; look not so pale. I tell you yet again, Banquo's buried; he cannot come out on's grave.

DOCTOR: Even so?

55 LADY MACBETH: To bed, to bed; there's knocking at the gate. Come, come, come, come, give me your hand. What's done cannot be undone. To bed, to bed, to bed.

[Exit.]

DOCTOR: Will she go now to bed?

GENTLEWOMAN: Directly.

60 DOCTOR: Foul whisperings are abroad. Unnatural deeds
Do breed unnatural troubles: infected minds
To their deaf pillows will discharge their secrets:
More needs she the divine than the physician.
God, God, forgive us all! Look after her;

LADY MACBETH: *Here is the smell of the blood still on my hands. All the perfumes of Arabia will not sweeten that smell on this little hand. Oh, oh, oh!*

DOCTOR: *What a burden she has! Her heart is sorely burdened.*

GENTLEWOMAN: *I would not keep such a heart in my bosom even to save the life of the whole body.*

DOCTOR: *Well, well, well—*

GENTLEWOMAN: *Pray God it is that, sir.*

DOCTOR: *This disease is beyond my practice. Yet I have known those who walk in their sleep and still died innocently in their beds.*

LADY MACBETH: *Wash your hands; put on your nightgown. Do not look so pale. I tell you yet again, Banquo's buried; he cannot come out of his grave.*

DOCTOR: *What?*

LADY MACBETH: *Get to bed. Get to bed. There's a knocking at the gate. Come, come, come, come; give me your hand. What's done cannot be undone. To bed, to bed, to bed.*

[Exit.]

DOCTOR: *Will she go now to bed?*

GENTLEWOMAN: *Directly.*

DOCTOR: *Foul whisperings are all around us. Unnatural deeds breed unnatural troubles, and infected minds will many times tell their secrets to their deaf pillows. She needs God's help more than the physician's. God, God, forgive us all! Look after her. Remove from her anything that could harm her but still watch her*

65   Remove from her the means of all annoyance,
      And still keep eyes upon her. So good night:
      My mind she has mated and amazed my sight:
      I think, but dare not speak.

GENTLEWOMAN: Good night, good doctor.

                                    [Exeunt.]

SCENE 2
The country near Dunsinane.

[Drum and colors. Enter Menteith, Caithness, Angus, Lennox, and
Soldiers.]

MENTEITH: The English power is near, led on by Malcolm,
      His uncle Siward, and the good Macduff.
      Revenges burn in them, for their dear causes
      Would to the bleeding and the grim alarm
5   Excite the mortified man.

ANGUS: Near Birnam Wood
      Shall we well meet them; that way are they coming.

CAITHNESS: Who knows if Donalbain be with his brother?

LENNOX: For certain, sir, he is not; I have a file
10   Of all the gentry. There is Siward's son
      And many unrough youths, that even now
      Protest their first of manhood.

MENTEITH: What does the tyrant?

closely. Good noght. I am absolutely amazed at these sights. I think I know what they mean, but I dare not speak of it.

GENTLEWOMAN: *Good night, good doctor.*

[Exit.]

SCENE 2

The country near Dunsinane.

[Drum and flags. Enter Menteith, Caithness, Angus, Lennox, and Soldiers.]

MENTEITH: *The English troops are near led on by Malcolm, his uncle Siward, and the good Macduff. Revenge burns in them; their just causes will lead many to join us in this bloody and gruesome undertaking.*

ANGUS: *Shall we meet them near Birnam Wood? They are coming that way.*

CAITHNESS: *Has anyone heard if Donalbain is with Malcolm's forces?*

LENNOX: *He certainly is not. I have a list of all the gentlemen. There are Siward's son and many untested youths who even now are entering manhood.*

MENTEITH: *What does Macbeth do?*

CAITHNESS: Great Dunsinane he strongly fortifies.
15   Some say he's mad; others, that lesser hate him,
    Do call it valiant fury: but, for certain,
    He cannot buckle his distemper'd cause
    Within the belt of rule.

ANGUS: Now does he feel
20   His secret murders sticking on his hands,
    Now minutely revolts upbraid his faith-breach;
    Those he commands move only in command,
    Nothing in love. Now does he feel his title
    Hang loose about him, like a giant's robe
25   Upon a dwarfish thief.

MENTEITH: Who then shall blame
    His pester'd senses to recoil and start,
    When all that is within him does condemn
    Itself for being there?

30 CAITHNESS: Well, march we on,
    To give obedience where 'tis truly owed.
    Meet we the medicine of the sickly weal,
    And with him pour we, in our country's purge,
    Each drop of us.

35 LENNOX: Or so much as it needs
    To dew the sovereign flower and drown the weeds.
    Make we our march towards Birnam

[Exeunt marching.]

CAITHNESS: *He strongly fortifies Great Dunsinane. Some say he's mad. Others, who hate him less, call it valiant fury. Certainly, though, he is losing control over his kingdom despite his own actions.*

ANGUS: *He now feels his secret murders sticking to his hands. Each tiny revolt blames his breach of faith. Those he commands move only because they are commanded, not because they love Macbeth. He now feels his title hang loosely about him, like a giant's robe would upon a dwarfish thief.*

MENTEITH: *Who can doubt his erratic behavior since every fiber of his being condemns itself for being there?*

CAITHNESS: *Well, we march on to give obedience where it is truly owed. We will meet Malcolm; his medicine and ours will cleanse this sickly country.*

LENNOX: *We will do what is needed to eliminate Macbeth and restore sovereignty to Scotland.*

[Exit marching.]

SCENE 3
Dunsinane. A room in the castle.

[Enter Macbeth, Doctor, and Attendants.]

MACBETH: Bring me no more reports; let them fly all!
   Till Birnam Wood remove to Dunsinane
   I cannot taint with fear. What's the boy Malcolm?
   Was he not born of woman? The spirits that know
5   All mortal consequences have pronounced me thus:
   "Fear not, Macbeth; no man that's born of woman
   Shall e'er have power upon thee." Then fly, false thanes,
   And mingle with the English epicures!
   The mind I sway by and the heart I bear
10   Shall never sag with doubt nor shake with fear.

[Enter a Servant.]

   The devil damn thee black, thou cream-faced loon!
   Where got'st thou that goose look?

SERVANT: There is ten thousand—

MACBETH: Geese, villain?

15 SERVANT: Soldiers, sir.

MACBETH: Go prick thy face and over-red thy fear,
   Thou lily-liver'd boy. What soldiers, patch?
   Death of thy soul! Those linen cheeks of thine
   Are counselors to fear. What soldiers, whey-face?

20 SERVANT: The English force, so please you.

MACBETH: Take thy face hence. *[Exit Servant.]*
   Seyton—I am sick at heart,
   When I behold—Seyton, I say!—This push

174

SCENE 3

Dunsinane. A room in the castle.

[Enter Macbeth, Doctor, and Attendants.]

MACBETH: *Do not bring me any more reports. Send the messengers away! Until Birnam Wood moves to Dunsinane, I shall not flinch with fear. What's the boy Malcolm? Was he not born of woman? The witches who know all things have told me specifically, "Fear not, Macbeth; no man who was born of woman shall ever have power over you." Then fly, false lords, and join the English forces! My mind and heart will never sag with doubt nor shake with fear.*

[Enter a Servant.]

May the devil kill you—you pasty-faced idiot! Where did you get that frightened look?

SERVANT: *There are ten thousand—*

MACBETH: *Geese, villain?*

SERVANT: *Soldiers, sir.*

MACBETH: *Go scratch your face and cover over the fear in your cheeks, you scared boy. What soldiers, clown? Death of your soul! Those white cheeks of yours show your fear. What soldiers, pale-face?*

SERVANT: *The English force, if it so please you.*

MACBETH: *Take your face away.* [Exit Servant.] *Seyton—I am sick at heart when I behold— Seyton, I say!—This impending fight will cheer me up forever or push me from the throne. I have lived*

25 Will cheer me ever or disseat me now.
I have lived long enough. My way of life
Is fall'n into the sear, the yellow leaf,
And that which should accompany old age,
As honor, love, obedience, troops of friends,
I must not look to have; but, in their stead,
30 Curses, not loud but deep, mouth-honor, breath,
Which the poor heart would fain deny and dare not.
Seyton!

[Enter Seyton.]

SEYTON: What's your gracious pleasure?

MACBETH: What news more?

35 SEYTON: All is confirm'd, my lord, which was reported.

MACBETH: I'll fight, 'til from my bones my flesh be hack'd.
Give me my armor.

SEYTON: 'Tis not needed yet.

MACBETH: I'll put it on.
40 Send out more horses, skirr the country round,
Hang those that talk of fear. Give me mine armor.
How does your patient, doctor?

DOCTOR: Not so sick, my lord,
As she is troubled with thick-coming fancies,
45 That keep her from her rest.

MACBETH: Cure her of that.
Canst thou not minister to a mind diseased,
Pluck from the memory a rooted sorrow,
Raze out the written troubles of the brain,
50 And with some sweet oblivious antidote
Cleanse the stuff'd bosom of that perilous stuff
Which weighs upon the heart?

176

long enough. *My aging life has become like the yellowed leaf before winter. The honor, love, obedience, and troops of friends which should be my due at my age will never be mine. Instead I hear whispered curses which I wish I could deny hearing, but dare not. Seyton*

[Enter Seyton and the doctor.]

SEYTON: *What is my lord's pleasure?*

MACBETH: *What additional news has come in?*

SEYTON: *All of that which was reported now is confirmed, my lord.*

MACBETH: *I'll fight until my flesh be hacked from my bones. Give me my armor.*

SEYTON: *It is not needed yet.*

MACBETH: *I'll put it on anyway. Send out more horses. Scour the whole country and hang those who talk of fear. Give me my armor. How does your patient, doctor?*

DOCTOR: *She is not so sick, my lord; but rather, she is troubled with hallucinations which keep her from her rest.*

MACBETH: *Cure her of that. Can you not minister to a diseased mind and pluck a hidden sorrow from her memory? Can you not erase the troubles of her brain with an antidote and cleanse her soul of all the problems which weigh upon her heart?*

DOCTOR: Therein the patient
　　Must minister to himself.

55　MACBETH: Throw physic to the dogs, I'll none of it.
　　Come, put mine armor on; give me my staff.
　　Seyton, send out. Doctor, the thanes fly from me.
　　Come, sir, dispatch. If thou couldst, doctor, cast
　　The water of my land, find her disease
60　And purge it to a sound and pristine health,
　　I would applaud thee to the very echo,
　　That should applaud again. Pull't off, I say.
　　What rhubarb, senna, or what purgative drug
　　Would scour these English hence? Hear'st thou of them?

65　DOCTOR: Ay, my good lord: your royal preparation
　　Makes us hear something.

MACBETH: Bring it after me.
　　I will not be afraid of death and bane
　　Till Birnam Forest come to Dunsinane.

70　DOCTOR: *[Aside.]* Were I from Dunsinane away and clear,
　　Profit again should hardly draw me here.

[Exeunt.]

DOCTOR: For things of that nature, the patient must heal to himself.

MACBETH: Throw your science to the dogs; I'll have none of it. Come, put my armor on; give me my lance. Seyton, send out. Doctor, the lords fly from me. Come, Seyton, quickly. If you could, doctor, study my country's problem, find her disease, and cleanse it so it is once again healthy; I would applaud you again and again. Pull it off, I say. What laxatives could flush these English from our lands? Do you hear about them?

DOCTOR: Yes, my good lord. Your royal preparations make us aware that something is about to happen.

MACBETH: Bring it after me. I will not be afraid of death and destruction until Birnam Forest comes to Dunsinane.

DOCTOR: [Aside.] If I can get away and clear from Dunsinane, no amount of money would draw me here again.

[Exit.]

SCENE 4
Country near Birnam Wood.

[Drum and colors. Enter Malcolm, old Siward and his Son, Macduff, Menteith, Caithness, Angus, Lennox, Ross, and Soldiers, marching.]

MALCOLM: Cousins, I hope the days are near at hand
    That chambers will be safe.

MENTEITH: We doubt it nothing.

SIWARD: What wood is this before us?

5   MENTEITH: The Wood of Birnam.

MALCOLM: Let every soldier hew him down a bough,
    And bear't before him: thereby shall we shadow
    The numbers of our host, and make discovery
    Err in report of us.

10   SOLDIERS: It shall be done.

SIWARD: We learn no other but the confident tyrant
    Keeps still in Dunsinane, and will endure
    Our setting down before't.

MALCOLM: 'Tis his main hope;
15   For where there is advantage to be given,
    Both more and less have given him the revolt,
    And none serve with him but constrained things
    Whose hearts are absent too.

MACDUFF: Let our just censures
20   Attend the true event, and put we on
    Industrious soldiership.

SCENE 4

Country near Birnam Wood.

[Drum and flags. Enter Malcolm, old Siward and his Son, Macduff, Menteith, Caithness, Angus, Lennox, Ross, and Soldiers, marching.]

MALCOLM: *Cousins, I hope the days are near at hand when our own bedrooms will be safe.*

MENTEITH: *We doubt it not.*

SIWARD: *What wood is this in front of us?*

MENTEITH: *The Wood of Birnam.*

MALCOLM: *Let every soldier chop down a bough of these evergreens and carry it in front of him. This way we shall camouflage the numbers of our army and make scouts err in reporting the number of our forces.*

SOLDIERS: *It shall be done.*

SIWARD: *We learn nothing except that the confident tyrant is barricaded in Dunsinane and will await a siege.*

MALCOLM: *It is his main hope. All advantages have swung to our cause, and no one serves him other than those who are forced.*

MACDUFF: *Judgment waits the outcome of the battle. Be ready to battle him.*

SIWARD: The time approaches
　　　That will with due decision make us know
　　　What we shall say we have and what we owe.
25　　Thoughts speculative their unsure hopes relate,
　　　But certain issue strokes must arbitrate;
　　　Towards which, advance the war.

[Exeunt Marching.]

SCENE 5
Dunsinane. Within the castle.

[Enter Macbeth, Seyton, and Soldiers, with drum and colors.]

MACBETH: Hang out our banners on the outward walls;
　　　The cry is still, "They come": Our castle's strength
　　　Will laugh a siege to scorn. Here let them lie
　　　Till famine and the ague eat them up.
5　　Were they not forced with those that should be ours,
　　　We might have met them dareful, beard to beard,
　　　And beat them backward home.
　　　　　　　　[A cry of women within.]
　　　What is that noise?

SEYTON: It is the cry of women, my good lord.

[Exit.]

10　MACBETH: I have almost forgot the taste of fears:
　　　The time has been, my senses would have cool'd
　　　To hear a night-shriek, and my fell of hair
　　　Would at a dismal treatise rouse and stir
　　　As life were in't: I have supp'd full with horrors;
15　　Direness, familiar to my slaughterous thoughts,
　　　Cannot once start me.

SIWARD: *The time approaches that will decide the outcome, giving us victory or defeat. We can speculate all we want about the future, but certain issues must be decided in battle. Therefore, let us march.*

[Exit marching.]

SCENE 5

Dunsinane. Within the castle.

[Enter Macbeth, Seyton, and Soldiers, with drum and colors.]

MACBETH: *Hang out our banners on the outward walls; the cry is still, "They come!" Our castle's strength will laugh with scorn at a siege. Let them lie in front of my castle until famine or fever eats them up. If their troops had not been reinforced with Scottish rebels, we might have met them beard to beard and beaten them back to England.*
[A cry of women within.]
What is that noise?

SEYTON: *It is the cry of women, my good lord.*

[Exit.]

MACBETH: *I have almost forgotten how fear tastes. At one time my senses would have chilled to hear a scream, and my hair would have stood on end at such a shriek. But now, I have experienced many horrors. Desperation, familiar to my murderous thoughts, can no longer startle me.*

183

[Re-enter Seyton.]

Wherefore was that cry?

SEYTON: The Queen, my lord, is dead.

MACBETH: She should have died hereafter;
20   There would have been a time for such a word.
        Tomorrow, and tomorrow, and tomorrow
        Creeps in this petty pace from day to day
        To the last syllable of recorded time;
        And all our yesterdays have lighted fools
25   The way to dusty death. Out, out, brief candle!
        Life's but a walking shadow, a poor player
        That struts and frets his hour upon the stage
        And then is heard no more. It is a tale
        Told by an idiot, full of sound and fury,
30   Signifying nothing.

[Enter a Messenger.]

Thou comest to use thy tongue; thy story quickly.

MESSENGER: Gracious my lord,
        I should report that which I say I saw,
        But know not how to do it.

35   MACBETH: Well, say, sir.

MESSENGER: As I did stand my watch upon the hill,
        I look'd toward Birnam, and anon, methought,
        The Wood began to move.

MACBETH: Liar and slave!

40   MESSENGER: Let me endure your wrath, if't be not so.
        Within this three mile may you see it coming;
        I say, a moving grove.

[Re-enter Seyton.]

What was that cry?

SEYTON: *The Queen, my lord, is dead.*

MACBETH: *She should have died at a later time; there would have been time for proper mourning. But time moves continually. It creeps slowly from day to day forever. All our days are spent, like a light, that only moves toward extinguishment or death. Out, out, brief candle! Life's only a shadowy figure, a poor actor that struts and frets his hour upon the stage and then is heard no more. It is a tale told by an idiot, full of sound and fury, signifying nothing.*

[Enter a Messenger.]

You come to use your tongue; quickly, tell your story.

MESSENGER: *My dear lord, I would report that which I say I saw, but I do not know how to tell it.*

MACBETH: *Well, sir, just say it.*

MESSENGER: *As I stood my watch upon the hill, I looked toward Birnam and thought the wood began to move.*

MACBETH: *Liar and slave!*

MESSENGER: *Let me endure your wrath if what I say is not true. Within these three miles you may see it coming; a moving grove, I say.*

MACBETH: If thou speak'st false,
Upon the next tree shalt thou hang alive,
45 Till famine cling thee; if thy speech be sooth,
I care not if thou dost for me as much.
I pull in resolution and begin
To doubt the equivocation of the fiend
That lies like truth. "Fear not, till Birnam Wood
50 Do come to Dunsinane," and now a wood
Comes toward Dunsinane. Arm, arm, and out!
If this which he avouches does appear,
There is nor flying hence nor tarrying here.
I 'gin to be aweary of the sun
55 And wish the estate o' the world were now undone.
Ring the alarum bell! Blow, wind! Come, wrack!
At least we'll die with harness on our back.

[Exeunt.]

MACBETH: *If you speak false, upon the next tree you will be hanged alive until you starve to death; if your speech is true, I don't care if you do the same to me. I pull in my resolve and begin to fear the deceptions of the witches whom I believed. "Fear not, till Birnam Wood come to Dunsinane," and now a wood does come toward Dunsinane. Arm, arm, and get ready! If what you say is indeed true, there is neither a way to flee, nor any hope in staying here. I begin to be weary of the light and wish the world would end. Ring the alarm! Blow, wind! Come, destruction! At least we'll die like soldiers.*

[Exit.]

SCENE 6
Dunsinane. Before the castle.

[Enter Malcolm, old Siward, Macduff, and their Army, with boughs. Drum and colors.]

MALCOLM: Now near enough; your leavy screens throw down,
  And show like those you are. You, worthy uncle,
  Shall, with my cousin, your right noble son,
  Lead our first battle. Worthy Macduff and we
5 Shall take upon's what else remains to do,
  According to our order.

SIWARD: Fare you well.
  Do we but find the tyrant's power tonight,
  Let us be beaten, if we cannot fight.

10 MACDUFF: Make all our trumpets speak; give them all breath,
  Those clamorous harbingers of blood and death.

[Exeunt.]

SCENE 6

Dunsinane. Before the castle.

[Enter Malcolm, old Siward, Macduff, and their Army, with boughs. Drum and colors.]

MALCOLM: *We are now near enough. Toss away your branches and reveal who you are. Worthy Siward and his son will lead us into our first attack. Macduff and I will split up the remaining duties according to our plan.*

SIWARD: *Farewell. If we face Macbeth's forces tonight, let us be beaten if we do not fight well.*

MACDUFF: *Make all our trumpets sound; fill them all with breath. They are the loud prophets of blood and death.*

[Exit.]

SCENE 7
Another part of the field.

[Enter Macbeth.]

MACBETH: They have tied me to a stake; I cannot fly,
  But bear-like I must fight the course. What's he
  That was not born of woman? Such a one
  Am I to fear, or none.

[Enter young Siward.]

5   YOUNG SIWARD: What is thy name?

MACBETH: Thou'lt be afraid to hear it.

YOUNG SIWARD: No, though thou call'st thyself a hotter name
  Than any is in hell.

MACBETH: My name's Macbeth.

10   YOUNG SIWARD: The devil himself could not pronounce a title
  More hateful to mine ear.

MACBETH: No, nor more fearful.

YOUNG SIWARD: Thou liest, abhorred tyrant; with my sword
  I'll prove the lie thou speak'st.
  [They fight, and young Siward is slain.]

15   MACBETH: Thou wast born of woman.
  But swords I smile at, weapons laugh to scorn,
  Brandish'd by man that's of a woman born.

[Exit.]

SCENE 7
Another part of the field.

[Enter Macbeth.]

MACBETH: *They have tied me to a stake, and I cannot flee. I must fight the course like a bear. Who is he that was not born of woman? Only someone like that am I to fear.*

[Enter young Siward.]

YOUNG SIWARD: *What is your name?*

MACBETH: *You would be afraid to hear it.*

YOUNG SIWARD: *No, even if you call yourself a hotter name than any who is in hell.*

MACBETH: *My name's Macbeth.*

YOUNG SIWARD: *The devil himself could not pronounce a title more hateful to my ear.*

MACBETH: *No, nor more fearful.*

YOUNG SIWARD: *O, you lie, hated tyrant. With my sword I'll prove it.*
                        [They fight, and young Siward is slain.]

MACBETH: *You were born of woman. But I smile at swords and laugh at weapons carried by any man who is born of a woman.*

                                        [Exit.]

[Alarums. Enter Macduff.]

MACDUFF: That way the noise is. Tyrant, show thy face!
    If thou be'st slain and with no stroke of mine,
20   My wife and children's ghosts will haunt me still.
    I cannot strike at wretched kerns, whose arms
    Are hired to bear their staves. Either thou, Macbeth,
    Or else my sword, with an unbatter'd edge,
    I sheathe again undeeded. There thou shouldst be;
25   By this great clatter, one of greatest note
    Seems bruited. Let me find him, fortune!
    And more I beg not.

[Exit. Alarums.]

[Enter Malcolm and old Siward.]

SIWARD: This way, my lord; the castle's gently render'd.
    The tyrant's people on both sides do fight,
30   The noble thanes do bravely in the war;
    The day almost itself professes yours,
    And little is to do.

MALCOLM: We have met with foes
    That strike beside us.

35 SIWARD: Enter, sir, the castle.

[Exeunt. Alarum.]

[Alarms. Enter Macduff.]

MACDUFF: *The noise is that way. Tyrant, show yourself! If you are killed by anyone but me, my family's ghosts will haunt me. I will not fight hired soldiers. It must be you, Macbeth, or else I will put my sword up without doing my duty. All this noise should announce your presence here. God, the only thing I ask is to let me find him.*

[Exit. Alarms.]

[Enter Malcolm and old Siward.]

SIWARD: *This way, my lord; the castle's easily taken. Scots fight on both sides, and the noble lords do brave deeds in the war. The fighting is almost over and there is little to do.*

MALCOLM: *We have even met foes who now fight on our side.*

SIWARD: *Enter the castle.*

[Exit. Alarm.]

SCENE 8
Another part of the field.

[Enter Macbeth.]

MACBETH: Why should I play the Roman fool and die
    On mine own sword? Whiles I see lives, the gashes
    Do better upon them.

[Enter Macduff.]

MACDUFF: Turn, hell hound, turn!

5   MACBETH: Of all men else I have avoided thee.
    But get thee back; my soul is too much charged
    With blood of thine already.

MACDUFF: I have no words:
    My voice is in my sword, thou bloodier villain
10   Than terms can give thee out!   *[They fight.]*

MACBETH: Thou losest labor.
    As easy mayst thou the intrenchant air
    With thy keen sword impress as make me bleed:
    Let fall thy blade on vulnerable crests;
15   I bear a charmed life, which must not yield
    To one of woman born.

MACDUFF: Despair thy charm,
    And let the angel whom thou still hast served
    Tell thee, Macduff was from his mother's womb
20   Untimely ripp'd.

MACBETH: Accursed be that tongue that tells me so,
    For it hath cow'd my better part of man!
    And be these juggling fiends no more believed,
    That palter with us in a double sense,
25   That keep the word of promise to our ear,
    And break it to our hope. I'll not fight with thee.

SCENE 8
Another part of the field.

[Enter Macbeth.]

MACBETH: *Why should I act like a Roman and commit suicide with my own sword? While I see live opponents, the cuts look better on them.*

[Enter Macduff.]

MACDUFF: *Turn, hellhound, turn!*

MACBETH: *I have avoided you more than anyone else. Stand back. My soul is already too much filled with the blood of your family.*

MACDUFF: *I have no words. My voice is in my sword, you bloodier villain than words can ever say!* [They fight.]

MACBETH: *You are wasting your strength. Your sharp sword can just as easily cut the air as make me bleed. Let your blade fall on vulnerable helmets. I bear a charmed life which cannot be lost to one of woman born.*

MACDUFF: *Despair your charm and let the devil that you serve tell you that I was born by Caesarean section.*

MACBETH: *Cursed be the tongue that tells me so, because it has made me cower in fear! I will never again believe those juggling witches who talk to us in double meaning and promise us the world only to crush all of our hopes. I'll not fight with you.*

MACDUFF: Then yield thee, coward,
    And live to be the show and gaze o' the time.
    We'll have thee, as our rarer monsters are,
30   Painted upon a pole, and underwrit,
    "Here may you see the tyrant."

MACBETH: I will not yield,
    To kiss the ground before young Malcolm's feet,
    And to be baited with the rabble's curse.
35   Though Birnam Wood be come to Dunsinane,
    And thou opposed, being of no woman born,
    Yet I will try the last. Before my body
    I throw my warlike shield! Lay on, Macduff,
    And damn'd be him that first cries, "Hold, enough!"

[Exeunt fighting. Alarums.]

[Retreat. Flourish. Enter, with drum and colors, Malcolm, old Siward, Ross, the other Thanes, and Soldiers.]

40   MALCOLM: I would the friends we miss were safe arrived.

SIWARD: Some must go off: and yet, by these I see,
    So great a day as this is cheaply bought.

MALCOLM: Macduff is missing, and your noble son.

ROSS: Your son, my lord, has paid a soldier's debt:
45   He only lived but till he was a man;
    The which no sooner had his prowess confirm'd
    In the unshrinking station where he fought,
    But like a man he died.

SIWARD: Then he is dead?

MACDUFF: *Then surrender, coward, and live to be exhibited and displayed. We'll have a sign made to be displayed over your head as we do for monsters—"Here may you see the tyrant."*

MACBETH: *I will not surrender, to kiss the ground under young Malcolm's feet or to be harassed by the rabble's curses. Though Birnam Wood came to Dunsinane and even though you were not "born" to woman, yet I will try one last time. In front of my body I throw my warlike shield! Let's go, Macduff, and damned be the warrior who first cries, "Hold, enough!"*

[Exit fighting. Alarms.]

[Retreat. Flourish. Enter, with drum and colors, Malcolm, old Siward, Ross, the other Thanes, and Soldiers.]

MALCOLM: *I hope the friends we miss are safe.*

SIWARD: *Some must be killed in war, and yet so great a day as this has been achieved at a minimal cost.*

MALCOLM: *Macduff is still missing, and so is your noble son.*

ROSS: *Your son, my lord, has paid a soldier's debt. He only lived until he reached manhood. No sooner had he achieved manhood and become a skilled warrior than he was killed.*

SIWARD: *Then he is dead?*

50 ROSS: Ay, and brought off the field. Your cause of sorrow
   Must not be measured by his worth, for then
   It hath no end.

SIWARD: Had he his hurts before?

ROSS: Ay, on the front.

55 SIWARD: Why then, God's soldier be he!
   Had I as many sons as I have hairs,
   I would not wish them to a fairer death.
   And so his knell is knoll'd.

MALCOLM: He's worth more sorrow,
60 And that I'll spend for him.

SIWARD: He's worth no more:
   They say he parted well and paid his score:
   And so God be with him! Here comes newer comfort.

[Re-enter Macduff, with Macbeth's head.]

MACDUFF: Hail, King! for so thou art. Behold where stands
65 The usurper's cursed head. The time is free.
   I see thee compass'd with thy kingdom's pearl
   That speak my salutation in their minds,
   Whose voices I desire aloud with mine:
   Hail, King of Scotland!

70 ALL: Hail, King of Scotland!   *[Flourish.]*

MALCOLM: We shall not spend a large expense of time
   Before we reckon with your several loves,
   And make us even with you. My thanes and kinsmen,
   Henceforth be Earls, the first that ever Scotland
75 In such an honor named. What's more to do,
   Which would be planted newly with the time,

198

Act V Scene 8

ROSS: *Yes, and brought off the field. Your grief will have no end if you measure it by his worth.*

SIWARD: *Had he his wounds in the front of his body?*

ROSS: *Yes, on the front.*

SIWARD: *Why then, let him be God's soldier! If I had as many sons as I have hairs, I would not wish them to a fairer death than this. And so we toll his death.*

MALCOLM: *He is worth more sorrow, and that I'll spend for him later.*

SIWARD: *He's worth no more. They say he died well and paid his score, and so God be with him! Here comes newer comfort.*

[Re-enter Macduff, with Macbeth's head.]

MACDUFF: *Hail, King, for you are now so. Behold the usurper's cursed head. The time is now free. I see you surrounded by our kingdom's finest who speak in their minds what I desire to say out loud—hail, King of Scotland!*

ALL: *Hail, King of Scotland!*   [Flourish.]

MALCOLM: *We shall not spend a large expense of time before we settle our debts to you. My lords and kinsmen, henceforth be Earls, the first that ever Scotland has so named or honored. We have*

As calling home our exiled friends abroad
That fled the snares of watchful tyranny,
Producing forth the cruel ministers
80 Of this dead butcher and his fiend-like queen,
Who, as 'tis thought, by self and violent hands
Took off her life; this, and what needful else
That calls upon us, by the grace of Grace
We will perform in measure, time, and place,
85 So thanks to all at once and to each one,
Whom we invite to see us crown'd at Scone.

[Flourish. Exeunt.]

more to do and will immediately begin to call home our exiled friends from abroad who fled the snares of this tyrant, his cruel ministers, and his fiendish queen. She is thought to have committed suicide. Whatever else we need to do, we will handle in the proper time, place, and measure. So thanks to all at once and to each one whom we invite to see us crowned at Scone.

[Flourish. Exit.]

STUDY GUIDE

Act I, Scene 1 - Three Witches

1. When are the three Witches to meet again, and for what purpose?

2. What do you suppose is suggested by the line, "Fair is foul, and foul is fair"?

Act I, Scene 2 - King Duncan and His Sons, Donalbain and Malcolm

1. What do we learn of Macbeth's courage and skill?

2. What is Macbeth's relationship to King Duncan?

3. Who have Macbeth and Banquo been fighting?

4. What does King Duncan tell Ross to do?

Act I, Scene 3 - Three Witches

1. As the scene begins, how does the conversation of the Witches strike you?

2. When Macbeth says, "So foul and fair a day I have not seen," to what is he referring? What could be the dramatic irony in this line?

3. Describe the physical appearance of the Witches.

4. What prophecies do the Witches make regarding Macbeth? How does he react?

5. What do the Witches see in the future for Banquo?

6. What does Banquo ask Macbeth about the experience?

7. As Banquo and Macbeth are discussing the prophecies, what news does Ross bring?

8. As the others talk, what does Macbeth's aside reveal about his thinking?

9. How does Banquo's comment support the "Fair is foul, foul is fair" theme?

10. What does Macbeth mean in his aside about two truths being prologue to the imperial theme?

11. What is Macbeth's emotional state when he hears the news?

12. To best understand Macbeth's feelings you must visualize what is happenings on stage. What is happening?

Act I, Scene 4 - King Duncan and His Sons

1. Why was the old Thane of Cawdor executed?

2. What is the meaning of the plant metaphor?

3. What news does the King impart to Macbeth and what is Macbeth's reaction to the news?

4. In his last speech in this scene, what does Macbeth reveal?

Act I, Scene 5 - Lady Macbeth

1. After Lady Macbeth finishes reading the letter, what fear about her husband does she express?

2. When Lady Macbeth says, "Hie thee hither," what is it that she plans to do?

3. How does the news about King Duncan's expected arrival affect Lady Macbeth? What is she planning?

4. Why does Lady Macbeth pray to be unsexed?

5. In what way does Lady Macbeth's advice to Macbeth relate to the "fair is foul" theme?

Act I, Scene 6 - King, Sons, and Entourage
1. What impression does Lady Macbeth make in this scene?

Act I, Scene 7 - Macbeth
1. After saying that if the deed is to be done it must be done quickly, what arguments does Macbeth raise for not doing it?

2. What does Macbeth finally conclude?

3. What does Macbeth decide before he speaks to Lady Macbeth?

4. What does Lady Macbeth say in an attempt to goad her husband into the murder?

5. Macbeth's response to Lady Macbeth about what a man may dare is frequently quoted. What is his meaning?

6. What is the point of Lady Macbeth's baby imagery?

Act II, Scene 1
1. What do you suppose is keeping Banquo from sleeping?

2. In his soliloquy after Banquo leaves, what does Macbeth tell the audience he sees? What could account for this apparition?

3. Describe Macbeth's mental/emotional state at this point?

Act II, Scene 2

1. What has Lady Macbeth done to the grooms?

2. Why does Lady Macbeth not commit the murder when she is in the room?

3. Macbeth, apparently troubled by the murder he has just committed, tells Lady Macbeth what he has seen and heard. She tells him to think on it no more. Why?

4. Macbeth's response is frequently quoted. What is the sense of this response?

5. In this scene, how does Lady Macbeth show herself to be stronger than her husband?

Act II, Scene 3

1. The Porter scene, or the "knocking at the gate," is debated by scholars, but many agree it is the typical comic relief scene seen in many of Shakespeare's plays. What do you suppose the dramatic point of a comic relief scene is? Why do you suppose the Porter's soliloquy is in prose rather than poetry? What lines contain the bawdy humor so often found in these scenes?

2. How is the theme of "a crime against nature" reinforced in this scene?

3. Why does Macduff refer to the scene of the murder as "a new Gorgon"?

4. Who is first suspected of the murder, and what happens to them?

5. Who are Malcolm and Donalbain, what do they suspect, and what decision do they make?

Act II, Scene 4

1. What additional natural (or unnatural) events further the "crime against nature theme"?

2. Who is suspected of having hired the grooms to kill Duncan? Why?

3. Why does Ross say, "'Gainst nature still"?

4. Why has Macbeth gone to Scone?

5. How did the crown happen to fall to Macbeth?

Act III, Scene 1

1. In his soliloquy, what suspicion and hope does Banquo reveal?

2. Macbeth seems to be very interested in Banquo's travel plans. Why do you suppose he is so interested?

3. The speech beginning "To be thus is nothing..." is often quoted. What is the meaning of that sentence? (You may have to read the rest of the soliloquy to see it.)

4. What is there in Banquo's character that makes Macbeth uneasy?

5. What is there in the situation with Banquo that particularly upsets Macbeth?

6. Although he has probably paid the murderers, how does Macbeth further motivate them?

7. What is it that Macbeth tells the murderers to do?

Act III, Scene 2

1. What is the meaning of Lady Macbeth's soliloquy in this scene?

2. In this scene, what is Macbeth's state of mind?

3. How does Macbeth show that his resolve has become stronger?

Act III, Scene 3

1. What happens at the ambush?

Act III, Scene 4

1. Irony is frequently a characteristic of Shakespeare's style as is his play on words. How is this technique demonstrated in the murderer's reply that Banquo is "safe" now?

2. Upon returning to the banquet table, what does Macbeth see and how does he respond? How do the others respond?

3. What is Lady Macbeth's reaction to Macbeth's hallucination?

4. How does Macbeth behave during the dinner, and what is the final result?

5. For what reason does Macduff's name come up?

6. What is Macbeth's next step?

Act III, Scene 5

1. Who is Hecate, and why is she angry?

2. What is Hecate's plan for Macbeth?

Act III, Scene 6

1. Why is Lennox so cautious in what he says? What, if anything, could be interpreted as a criticism of Macbeth?

2. Where has Macduff gone? Why?

3. What is Macbeth's response to these developments?

Act IV, Scene 1

1. What is the first apparition, and of what does it warn Macbeth?

2. What is the second apparition, and what is its comment?

3. What, after this, does Macbeth resolve?

4. What is the third apparition, and what is its message?

5. Pleased with the information, what one further thing does Macbeth desire to know and what is the answer he gets?

6. What news does Lennox give to Macbeth?

7. What is Macbeth's response to Lennox's news?

8. What is Macbeth's resolve at the end of this scene? How is it different from his previous actions?

Act IV, Scene 2

1. Why does Lady Macduff think Macduff's flight is unnatural?

2. What is Ross's response to Lady Macduff's assertions?

3. Since Macduff has fled and is not dead, why does Lady Macduff tell her son that he is dead?

4. How does Macduff's son know that his father isn't dead?

Act IV, Scene 3

1. What suspicion of Macduff does Malcolm voice?

2. How do Malcolm's comments about Macbeth echo the "fair is foul" theme?

3. What is it that makes Malcolm suspicious of Macduff's motives?

4. To what does Malcolm attribute his wariness of Macduff?

5. What is Macduff's response?

6. Malcolm reveals that he is more lustful, cruel, and avaricious than Macbeth, and he concludes by asking whether such a man is fit to govern. What is Macduff's response?

7. What is Malcolm's next admission?

8. After Malcolm tells Ross about Lord Siward and his 10,000 men preparing to leave for Scotland, what information does Ross give to Macduff?

9. How is Macduff's great grief conveyed?

10. What is Macduff's response when Malcolm says, "Dispute it like a man"?

11. What is Macduff's resolve?

Act V, Scene 1

1. Describe what the doctor observes.

2. Why does the doctor conclude that Lady Macbeth needs more help than a physician can give her?

Act V, Scene 2

1.   Whose side are Lennox, Angus, Menteith, and Caithness on?

2.   What do the above say of the men that Macbeth commands?

Act V, Scene 3

1.   What is Macbeth's lament in his "my way of life is fallen into the sear..." speech?

2.   What is Lady Macbeth's condition, and how does Macbeth believe it can be cured?

Act V, Scene 4

1.   What tactical strategy does Malcolm take?

Act V, Scene 5

1.   In reaction to the news that Lady Macbeth is dead, Macbeth delivers his most famous soliloquy. What does it mean?

2.   What alarming news does the messenger bring?

3.   In lines 42-44, what does Macbeth recognize and how does it fit in with the "fair is foul" theme?

Act V, Scene 7

1.   As bad as things look for Macbeth, why does he still scorn all his opponents?

2.   What is the meaning of Malcolm's statement that Macbeth's men "fight on both sides"?

Act V, Scene 8

1. What information does Macduff tell Macbeth that makes him frightened?

2. What is Macbeth's response to Macduff's news?

3. Why does Macbeth quickly change his mind about fighting?

4. On what note does the play end?

SIDE *by* SIDES

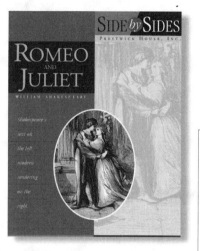

Our Complete Teacher's Kits Make Great Literature Accessible to ALL Your Students

EACH STUDENT LEARNS HOW TO UNDERSTAND AND LOVE LITERATURE DIFFERENTLY. Some learn best through short answer questions; some through preparing for tests; others through personal response questions; many through group and individual activities; and some learn best visually.

Writing and preparing dozens of different activities, essays, tests, and response questions is the most time-consuming, and sometimes most tedious, part of teaching. For a unique curriculum and to give you a wide variety of reproducible materials, we have combined our Teaching Units, Activity Packs, Response Journals, and, when available, our Headlines in one low-priced package that gives you everything you need to teach to all your students.

Perfect for New Teachers!

Activity Packs
These reproducibles are designed to guide student exploration of literature through cooperative learning techniques, map making, investigation of character-ization, literary terms, dramatizations, letter writing, and more. Separately, Activity Packs are **$34.95**.

Teaching Units
Complete Units, with educational objectives, comprehension and essay questions, literary terms, vocabulary, a multiple choice and essay test, and plot–and theme–level questions with answers to stress daily reading. Separately, Teaching Units are **$29.99**.

Response Journals
We present students with a series of writing prompts designed to approach the works from a more personal perspective. Students are expected to write letters of advice, keep a journal as if they were a character from the book, relate the plot to their own lives, and more. Separately, Response Journals are **$19.95**.

Headlines
We present literary works in the style of modern tabloids to pique student interest. For each book, we present the front page from three issues of an imaginary newspaper appropriate to the setting in an attractive poster that is perfect to complement the teaching of these books. Separately, Headlines are **$18.99**.

Complete Teacher's Kits without Headlines

IPWHC19	*The Education of Little Tree*	$74.95
IPWHC9	*The Call of the Wild*	$74.95
IPWHC10	*The Red Badge of Courage*	$74.95
IPWHC11	*The Catcher in the Rye*	$74.95
IPWHC12	*The Outsiders*	$74.95
IPWHC13	*Frankenstein*	$74.95
IPWHC14	*The House on Mango Street*	$74.95
IPWHC15	*The Old Man and the Sea*	$74.95
IPWHC16	*Holes*	$74.95
IPWHC17	*Hatchet*	$74.95
IPWHC18	*Slam!*	$74.95
IPWHC20	*Narrative of the Life of Frederick Douglass*	$74.95
IPWHC23	*The Adventures of Tom Sawyer*	$74.95
IPWHC26	*Fahrenheit 451*	$74.95

Complete Teacher's Kits with Headlines

IPWHC1	*Macbeth*	$84.95
IPWHC2	*Romeo and Juliet*	$84.95
IPWHC3	*The Adventures of Huckleberry Finn*	$84.95
IPWHC4	*Lord of the Flies*	$84.95
IPWHC5	*Of Mice and Men*	$84.95
IPWHC6	*The Great Gatsby*	$84.95
IPWHC7	*To Kill a Mockingbird*	$84.95
IPWHC8	*Julius Caesar*	$84.95
IPWHC21	*Hamlet*	$84.95
IPWHC22	*A Midsummer Night's Dream*	$84.95
IPWHC25	*A Separate Peace*	$84.95
IPWHC27	*The Crucible*	$84.95

PRESTWICK HOUSE, INC
"Everything for the English Classroom!"

New titles are constantly being added. Call or visit our website for a current listing.

Toll-free 1-800-932-4593 • Fax 1-888-718-9333 • Website: www.prestwickhouse.com